JONATHAN COUSER

The GENUINE Advantage

A Gameplan for Thriving Together—at Work, at Home, in Life. One Relationship at a Time.

Thanks to my wife Krissy, kids Owen, Eli, Evan, Jenna, and Sofia for years of support. It has been a long road learning how to run differently, they have seen it all and loved me through it. My wonderful editorial partner Christine Carter was the most generous professional I could have hoped to work with. And God for seeking me when I was content doing my own thing. He never gives up the pursuit.

.

Contents

Foreword

"Jonathan Couser has captured a truth I've spent twenty years learning: Success isn't just about achieving more—it's about how we get there and who we get there with."

As founder of a software development firm recognized as a Best Place to Work, I've always believed that culture is the backbone of sustainable growth. What makes *The GENUINE Advantage* stand out is how Jonathan turns this belief into a practical roadmap. The GENUINE framework isn't just thoughtful—it's usable. Whether you're leading a team or a family, it gives clear language to principles I lived out intuitively but never articulated well.

I especially appreciated how Jonathan bridges work and home life. So many leadership books treat those domains as separate, but the same principles that create trust in the workplace also strengthen the relationships that matter most. For years, my company operated on the belief that sick days didn't need to be "earned," that personal challenges deserved support, not suspicion. These weren't perks—they were expressions of who we wanted to be. Jonathan's framework validated what I'd discovered through experience and showed me how to teach it to others.

I met Jonathan when Switchbox partnered with a Fortune 20 company where he worked. What began as a vendor-client relationship became a friendship built on shared values about people, leadership, and meaningful work. Seeing those principles now distilled into this book feels both familiar and inspiring.

If you sense something important is missing—at work, at home, or within yourself—Jonathan offers not only insight but a path forward. I highly recommend this book to anyone building something worth sustaining.

This book is for people who sense that something important is missing—at work, at home, or simply within themselves. Jonathan offers not only insight, but a path forward. I highly recommend the book to aspiring leaders and business veterans.

Joel Stephens - Founder, Switchbox Inc. and Best Places to Work Recipient

Advanced Praise for The GENUINE Advantage

"The GENUINE Advantage framework is one of the most practical, actionable guides I've seen for building trust, strengthening connections, and creating a culture where excellence becomes sustainable. This isn't another leadership theory; it's a relational operating system every CEO should master."

—Brand Newland, CEO Goldfinch Healthcare, Husband, Mentor

"No matter the roles we hold—spouse, parent, child, leader, follower, or friend—we all need help cutting through the noise to rediscover the importance and value of authentic human connection. GENUINE Advantage serves as a trusted guide, leading us on a path toward giving our best selves to those around us.

—Matt Zelnik, Veteran, County Agency Executive, Husband, Father, Mentor

"The GENUINE Advantage exposes the lie that working harder will eventually give us everything we want—a mindset that has exhausted souls and fractured families. This book offers not just a better way, but practical tools to live it out in every area of life."

—Josh Taylor, Founding Pastor, Bright City Church (Ohio). Husband, Father, Mentor

"The GENUINE Advantage delivers the rare approach that feels both practical for business purposes and deeply human. This is a must-read for anyone who wants to build a business that succeeds because it stays true to what matters most."

—Stan Nagel, Retired HR Executive, Husband, Father, Grandfather, Mentor

1

Author's Note:

And years later, looking back, John would put it this way:

This book is my attempt to capture in a helpful way what I have learned as I traveled the road of life as a successful executive, spouse, parent, and community leader. It is a game plan for building the relationships you are designed to have and achieving the success you desire.

I lived the life of someone who achieved amazing wins. However, the results left me feeling empty and unsatisfied. Eventually, I arrived at a simple conclusion: Life is not just about what you achieve, but who you achieve life with. It's about living in a way that leaves a legacy worth repeating, not deleting. This fable is created from all the years I've spent living, researching, and practicing what it means to win in a way that creates thriving communities and develops future leaders.

I've tested every assumption I once made about leadership, family, faith, and success. I devoured the research, including:

- Harvard's 80-year study showing that relationships, not résumés, predict lifelong happiness.
- Business research, such as Gallup's data proving that people don't quit jobs, they quit bosses who don't connect.
- Hundreds of books, including Brené Brown's studies on vulnerability and trust; Jim Collins's work on leaders who last.

- Thousands of hours of podcasts on life, relationships, science, society, and leadership.

I saw the same theme echoing everywhere: Human connection is not optional for thriving. Positive relationships are the unexplainable results that everyone is longing to achieve. And healthy, GENUINE interactions, as I will label them in this book, are the foundational steps everyone is trying to figure out so they can intentionally achieve positive, healthy relationships. Strong relationships are the engine of loyalty, the glue that holds families together, the fuel that drives thriving cultures, and the key to achieving great results in all aspects of life.

I didn't just read about it all, I tested out the experiments in my daily life. I risked moving at a different pace when the Critic, my inner negative voice, kept me in fear of failing, telling me speed was needed for survival. I started listening when remaining silent made me feel weak. I tried generosity when self-reliance seemed safer. Some attempts failed. Some backfired. I lost opportunities because I chose presence over performance. But I also began to see something new: The very traits the world called soft were the traits that most consistently led to my success and building winning teams. The extra parts of life you would get to if you "had time" were the most valuable priorities you'd need for success.

I worked on making changes based on valuable insights, like learning to give and receive help (generosity), identifying a core set of values that enable you to show up the same anywhere, instead of having to switch into different masks (integrity), and being fully attentive (engaged) in the moment, instead of constantly pushing the boundaries of your ability to multitask. These are three of the seven principles you will be introduced to in this book.

Over decades in boardrooms and breakrooms, at ballfields and in my own living room, I practiced and refined what I now call "The GENUINE relationships advantage." It is based on seven principles, not hacks, not slogans, but actionable principles, that this book will describe as "batons" that you can use with people even when everything else seems to be falling apart. I've seen them work across continents, companies, congregations, and kitchens. I've seen burned-out executives rediscover their families, skeptical managers rebuild trust with their teams, and ordinary men and women carry these principles into spaces I'll never step foot in. The results are almost always the same: Unrivaled success that lasts beyond the individual and healthy environments that benefit everyone involved.

This book isn't a theory. It's a field guide born out of failure, tested in the real world, sharpened by scars. I offer an in-depth answer to why success can sometimes feel empty, lonely, and unsatisfying.

If you've ever heard your internal Critic's voice the way I did and believed what that voice was telling you- *that your worth is in the hours you put in, that strength is in the mask you wear, and that relationships are merely optional,* then this book is for you. It's about discovering the true way you were meant to run the race of life all along. The one where the goal isn't running alone but reaching the finish line together.

2

The Genuine Advantage: It Didn't Start This Way

John had always believed he was the kind of leader people wanted to follow. He was first to enter the office and the last to leave. He hit every target, led every meeting with precision, and made sure deadlines were never missed. He wore his long hours like a badge of honor, proof that no one could outwork him. His team respected his work ethic, or at least, he thought they did.

In truth, John had been shaped by a set of beliefs since his teenage years. His father, a man of few words, used to tell him, "Hard work fixes everything. If you're tired, keep going. If others doubt you, prove them wrong." Those words had been lodged deep inside him. Every promotion, every late night, every missed dinner at home, he quietly justified as sacrifices for a greater good. He believed leadership meant showing people that nothing would stop him.

But even as he stacked up the wins, another voice tagged along. The one that whispered in the quiet moments, *"If you slow down, you'll lose. If you say no, they'll replace you. If you show weakness, they'll walk right past you."* He never said it out loud, but he lived as if it were true. That sharp, demanding, and unrelenting voice had a name he wouldn't give it until years later... The Critic.

The year his company launched its first employee opinion survey, John couldn't wait to see the results. He expected glowing praise. Appreciation for his commitment, admiration for his drive, and perhaps even words like 'inspiring' or 'visionary'.

Instead, what he read knocked the breath out of him.

"John doesn't listen."

"He's always busy but never present."

"I don't feel like he knows me at all."

"Work gets done, but it doesn't feel like we're a team."

Page after page, the feedback cut deeper. It was like staring into a mirror that didn't match the image he carried in his mind. John closed his office door and stared at the ceiling, heat rising in his chest. He thought to himself, "How could this be? I've given everything. I've worked harder than anyone. Isn't that good leadership?"

The Critic slipped in, quick as ever: *They don't appreciate you. They don't understand what it takes. Just keep pushing forward.*

A knock on his door interrupted the spiral. Stan, his boss, stepped in holding a folder. He was a calm, matter-of-fact kind of leader who didn't waste words.

"John," Stan began, "you know I value the work you're doing. Numbers are strong. Results are strong. But I've read the same survey you just did. And it's clear your people don't feel connected to you."

John sat up straighter, defensive. "Connected? They respect me. They know I'm pushing just as hard as they are."

Stan shook his head. "Respect and connection aren't the same thing. I can't put my finger on it, but something's missing. And if you don't figure it out, it's going to limit you. You can drive results, but you won't build loyalty. And without loyalty, results don't last. In my experience under this type of leadership, eventually everyone burns out, even the leader."

He left the words hanging, then tapped the folder against his palm. "You've got potential to go further here. But if this doesn't change, you won't."

And just like that, Stan left. No instructions, no map, no clear path forward. Just the truth: Something wasn't working, and John would have to figure out what it was if he wanted to keep succeeding.

John sat frozen, staring at the survey comments as if they might rearrange themselves into something more palatable. In the glass of his office window, he saw his own reflection: A man in his early forties, tie slightly askew, eyes tired from nights that stretched too late. For the first time in years, he wondered if all his effort had bought him less than he imagined.

That night, still reeling, John's phone rang. It was his wife.

"Did you ever call the school about Sarah's conference? I just found out it was this morning. I thought you said you'd handle it."

John closed his eyes. He had meant to. He had even written it on a sticky note and stuck it to the side of his monitor. But in the whirlwind of deadlines, meetings, and the looming survey results, it had slipped. "I… I didn't," he admitted.

Silence on the other end. Then: "John, this matters. She matters. I can't keep being the one who picks up everything you drop."

He wanted to argue in defense and list the hours he'd spent wrestling with his son, the Saturdays he'd given to volunteering at the food pantry, the late-night grocery runs he made so his wife didn't have to go, the science project he helped glue together last week after an exhausting day at work. He wasn't absent. He was trying to be everywhere, for everyone.

His mind filled with the unspoken defense: Doesn't anyone see how much I'm doing? Why does it feel like no one appreciates me?

But the truth pressed down heavier than the words. He hadn't followed through. And this wasn't the first time.

Later that night, when Sarah padded into the kitchen in her pajamas, she glanced at him across the counter and said casually, "It's okay, Dad. I didn't think you'd make it to my school anyway." She wasn't angry. She was simply resigned. Somehow, that was worse.

Now, in the span of a single week, John had been told four things he couldn't ignore:

- His employees didn't feel connected to him.
- His boss didn't know what was missing, only that it was limiting.

- His wife was tired of carrying the weight of his broken commitments.
- His daughter shared that she didn't expect him to show up at her events.

The message was unmistakable: People might respect what he did, but they couldn't count on who he was.

That night, lying awake in bed, John admitted the truth to himself:

He wasn't failing because of his lack of effort. He was failing because of the way he was running this race called life. He may have had lots of wins, but he certainly wasn't winning.

The house was silent except for the hum of the air conditioner. He stared at the ceiling, a whisper of unease rising inside him. He thought of his office, the endless deadlines, the empty desks after his team had gone home, the dark windows reflecting his own weary face as he worked late. He recalled Sarah's words, casual but cutting, "I didn't think you'd come anyway."

He had climbed the ladder of success, but if he kept climbing this way, he'd end up at the top alone.

And then, almost like a whisper in the dark, a different question surfaced, and it was one he couldn't shake: 'What if real success wasn't about doing more, but about engaging more deeply in the right things?'

He didn't yet know what those "right things" were, or how to find them.

But he knew this much: Something had to change.

3

Years Later... The First Meeting

The café was full of its usual Friday hum. Cups clinking, grinders hissing, the mingled aroma of dark roast and warm croissants hanging in the air. John liked the noise. In a strange way, it reminded him that life was always happening all around, whether you slowed down to notice or not. For years, he had been too busy rushing past it. Now, he paid more attention.

He glanced up as Daniel entered, scanning the crowded room until his eyes landed on John. Daniel looked sharp, wearing a clean suit and jacket, his hair neatly combed, but his eyes gave him away. They carried the weariness of someone running too hard in too many directions, the same weary look John used to see in the mirror.

"Thanks for meeting me," Daniel said as he slid into the booth. He sounded both relieved and restless, like a man who didn't yet know he needed help. "Paul said you'd understand. He told me you once helped him when he was going through something similar. He insists I need something, and he says you know just what that is, which is great, because I am clueless."

John smiled at the memory. Paul, a shared friend, had once been in the same place: On the brink of burning out, trying to hold together his construction business and marriage while constantly proving his success everywhere at once- all the time. He remembered late-night phone calls, long silences over coffee, and the look of recognition in Paul's eyes when he finally realized he couldn't carry it all alone.

"Paul's a good man," John said. "If he thought we should sit down, then I'm glad you called."

Daniel nodded, almost defensively, as if embarrassed by his own need. "I guess I'm just… stuck. Everyone tells me I should be grateful. I've got a new promotion, three beautiful kids, and plenty of wins on the scoreboard. But honestly? I feel like I'm always on the brink of being found out that I am really just barely holding it all together."

As Daniel spoke, his phone buzzed on the table, vibrating every few seconds like a metronome marking his stress. Notifications stacked up in red banners across the screen. John gestured toward it with a half-smile. "You can put that away. You won't need it here."

Daniel hesitated, then reluctantly flipped the phone over.

"You said on the phone you're feeling stretched thin," John began. "Tell me what's going on."

Daniel leaned back, exhaling as if finally letting some of the pressure out. "I feel like I'm supposed to be three people at once. At work, they want me to be available 24/7. At home, my wife just had our third baby, and she needs me more than ever. And personally, I don't want to lose myself. I still want to get ahead, to build something, and achieve my goals."

He rubbed his temples, voice low. "I keep hearing people say I have it all. That I should 'feel great about my life.' But I don't know, all I see are opportunities to keep racing after more. To keep striving to win a race where the finish line always seems to be moving further away, no matter how fast, far, or hard I run. I am not sure when I will reach the actual finish line, but I am certain I can't keep this pace."

John let the silence breathe. He remembered the sting of the survey years ago, his wife's disappointment when he missed Sarah's school conference, the ache of trying to be everywhere and ending up nowhere fully present. He remembered how empty it felt to win at work and lose at home, or to win at home but then feel like it meant falling behind at work.

Finally, he leaned in. "Daniel, let me tell you something I wish someone had told me earlier. You can have it all… but you can't have everything."

Daniel frowned. "That sounds like wordplay."

John shook his head gently. "No. It's the difference between exhaustion and clarity. Between chasing every opportunity and engaging deeper in the right ones. The life you want isn't out of reach. But it will require a shift, not in how much you do, but in how you choose to run the race."

Daniel studied him, arms crossed like a shield, but his eyes gave him away. They showed hunger. The same hunger John had when Stan told him something was missing.

"So how do I figure that out?" Daniel asked.

John smiled. "That's the work. It's not about finding more time. It's about becoming more intentional with the time you already have. If you don't learn to choose, others will choose for you, and you will find their wisdom isn't always a good match for where you want to go."

Daniel leaned forward, about to press further, when a voice rang out from the pastry counter.

"Daniel! Hey, did you ever send the slides for Sunday's service?"

Daniel's head jerked up. A young man from church was waving. Daniel's face drained of color.

"Oh no," he muttered. He gave a quick smile and a wave back. "Yeah — I'll take care of it right after this."

Almost on cue, his phone buzzed again. Daniel grabbed it, thumb flying across the screen as he muttered, "I'm sorry — I've got to run. I didn't realize I'd dropped the ball on something else."

John nodded slowly. "It's all right. We'll pick this back up."

Daniel rushed out the door, already tapping furiously on his phone in one hand while juggling a coffee cup in the other with his keys dangling dangerously between his fingertips.

John sat back and watched through the window as Daniel disappeared into the blur of rushing bodies on the sidewalk. The café's noise swelled around him: The hiss of the espresso machine, the crash of dishes, the laughter of strangers.

For a moment, John just sat in the hum, unmoving. He knew exactly where Daniel's road would lead him, because he, too, had sprinted along it. And he also knew the hope Daniel couldn't yet see: There was another way. A better way. A more genuine way to run.

He took a sip of his cooling coffee and whispered almost to himself, "We'll get there."

4

Detour: Lunch with Mark

Daniel spotted him instantly. You couldn't miss Mark. Same confident stride as in college, same sharp smile. But now it came with a tailored suit, shiny cuff links, and sunglasses that probably cost more than Daniel's monthly car payment.

"Danny boy!" Mark's voice carried across the restaurant. Heads turned. Mark thrived on it. He clapped Daniel on the back and slid into the booth across from him.

"Sorry, I'm late. The business breakfast ran long. You know how it is, Tokyo time zone one day, New York the next. It never stops, so neither do I."

Daniel smiled politely. He'd seen the Instagram posts: The skyline views, the luxury hotels, the champagne toasts. Mark's life always looked big. Too big to ignore.

Mark ordered without looking at the menu, rattling off something in French to the waiter. Then he leaned in. "So, how's the life of a family man treating you?"

Daniel hesitated. "It's… good. Hard, sometimes. The kids don't really sleep, and work's picking up since my promotion. I feel like I'm constantly behind."

Mark grinned. "That's because you are. Look, you've got to decide, are you playing for comfort or for scale? I travel 200 days a year. My wife complains sometimes, sure. But hey, this is the grind. This is what pays off."

He tapped his brand-new Rolex watch. "This? Paid for in two small client deals. My kid will thank me later when he can go to any school he wants."

Daniel shifted in his seat. He remembered John's words from the café just a few days earlier: "You can have it all, but you can't have everything." But here was Mark, living proof, or so it seemed, that you could have everything if you worked hard enough.

Mark leaned back, stretching like he owned the room. "And don't feel guilty about missing bedtime stories, man. Kids don't remember that stuff. They remember the vacations, the cars, the big moves. That's what makes an impression."

Daniel forced a smile, but inside, something twisted. He wanted to believe Mark. He wanted freedom, success, and confidence. But he also heard John's calm voice in the back of his mind: "Engage deeper in the right things."

"Actually," Daniel said carefully, "I've been talking to someone. A guy named John. He's older and has been through a lot. Paul from our men's group connected us."

Mark smirked. "John? The sage type? Let me guess, telling you to slow down, be present, all that feel-good stuff?"

Daniel shrugged. "He didn't really tell me anything. He said something about having it all but not having everything, or something like that. He makes it sound like success isn't about running harder, further, or faster; it's about running after your results differently. Mark chuckled, swirling his drink. "That's cute. But there's only one way you get all this, he pointed his finger up and down at his clothes and all around the people in the exclusive restaurant. The race doesn't change because you want to slow down or have a different balance. Trust me, Danny, if you want to win, you've got to keep the pedal to the floor."

The waiter returned with Mark's order, something elegant and plated like art. Daniel barely touched his sandwich and fries.

As Mark launched into a story about closing a deal in Dubai, Daniel nodded along, but his mind was elsewhere. Two voices were forming a tug-of-war inside him:

- John's steady reminder: "You can have it all... but you can't have everything."
- Mark's confident boast: "You've got to keep the pedal to the floor."

Daniel smiled at the right moments and laughed at the right jokes. But when they stood to leave, he felt more unsettled than when he arrived.

Walking back to his car, he pulled out his phone and scrolled through Mark's photos: The private jet selfies, the rooftop cocktails, the perfect smiles. It all looked flawless.

And yet, a quiet question rose in him, uninvited: 'If it's really the best way... why does winning feel a lot less awesome than I thought it would? Why does winning feel exhausting instead of fulfilling?'

Post-Lunch Reflection — The Tension at Home

That evening, Daniel sat slouched on the couch, his phone glowing in his hand. Mark's Instagram feed was still open, crystal-clear shots of Dubai skyscrapers, champagne flutes clinking in first-class cabins, his three-year-old son grinning beside a new sports car in front of the family's garage.

Rachel moved around the living room, folding a stack of laundry into neat piles. She glanced at Daniel, then at the kids sprawled on the floor, crayons scattered as they colored. "You've been quiet since you got home," she said casually.

Daniel didn't look up. "Just tired."

But she noticed the flick of his thumb, the glossy images reflecting in his eyes. "That's Mark again, isn't it?"

Daniel shifted uncomfortably. "Yeah. He... he's doing well. Really well."

Rachel sat down across from him with a basket of laundry settled in her lap. "Daniel, he's been chasing that life since college. Private jets. Deals at midnight. You always said you didn't want that. You wanted a family. You wanted presence."

The mention of college coincided with Rachel's old sketchbook catching his eye; it sat on a shelf, a thin layer of dust softening its once-bright cover.

He remembered when it rarely left her hands during those late nights in their first apartment. Rachel would be hunched over the kitchen table, charcoal smudges on her wrist as she worked through another project for art school.

They married young, both brimming with dreams and more passion than money. He had charged into business with a head full of ambition, while she had filled their home with color and canvas.

When their daughter was born, Rachel had told him it was just a pause. "I'll pick it up again when things settle," she'd said, laying her brushes aside to make room for diapers and late-night feedings. Then came their son, and later the baby, each one, another beautiful reason to put her career temporarily on hold.

Rachel hadn't stopped creating altogether. She gave lessons to neighborhood kids at the dining table, teaching them how to let watercolors bleed or how to see the curve of a face instead of the flatness of a page. But Daniel knew those were fragments, not the future she once imagined. She had sacrificed a lot for their family, not because she had to, but because she believed the investment mattered. He realized she hadn't just paused her art for the family. She'd paused it because she believed the season wasn't over yet. She hadn't quit. She was waiting. Some called their approach traditional, others called it outdated, but for them, it worked. Each of them made an equal but different sacrifice, or so he thought, but maybe he was seeing things all wrong.

Daniel turned back to Rachel and swallowed hard. "I did, and I do, but he has both. Look at his social media feed. There it is: Wife, son, and sports car. He flipped to the next picture: A private jet, and the next was snorkeling with sea turtles. What if I'm wrong? What if I sold myself short? Mark has everything: Money, freedom, influence, and a family. And I'm here... trying to juggle a job that drains me and a family I'm not sure I'm showing up for well enough."

Rachel's voice softened. "And what do you think it costs him?"

He hesitated. He remembered Mark's words: "Kids don't remember bedtime stories." He thought of Rachel's sketchbook that she hadn't touched in years, gathering dust on the shelf. He thought of his son Ethan tugging his sleeve last week, asking him to play trucks, and the way he'd snapped: "Not now!"

Rachel leaned closer, her eyes steady. "I don't need private jets, Daniel. The kids don't either. We need you. Here. Not half-scrolling through someone else's life. Not double-checking that you've read every email. Not second-guessing whether your life is enough." Her words landed with a quiet weight. Daniel's phone dimmed in his hand, Mark's perfect life fading into a black screen. Across the room, his daughter giggled at something Ethan had drawn, holding the paper up proudly.

For a moment, his question cut through the haze in his mind: "Which life do I really want? The one that looks impressive on a screen, or the one sitting right here in front of me?"

Daniel set the phone face down on the table. He still felt torn between two voices, both confident but in totally different ways. John's confidence was calm and reassuring, like he had something he wanted to share with Daniel, but only when Daniel was ready. Mark's confidence felt more like a challenge to Daniel's existence. Mark had bravado and was completely confident he was winning the race, while Daniel needed to step up and start running harder because, right now, Daniel was falling behind.

Just then, another voice entered the conversation; it was his internal Critic, always quick to point out the gap between who Daniel was and who he believed he was supposed to be. The Critic left no doubt how he felt about the differences in confidence styles, and he was all in on Mark. The Critic made it clear, *"If Mark is the measuring stick for winning, you aren't just losing, you are getting lapped in the race."*

5

A Blow to the Foundation

A week later, Daniel came home exhausted from another week of running fast, hard, and towards a finish line that kept moving. He dropped his keys onto the counter. The clink on the counter was sharper than he meant, but it matched the weight pressing in on him. He hadn't even taken off his jacket, but already the house felt heavy, the air thicker than the brisk, humid evening he had just left outside.

From the kitchen came a familiar call: "Did you ever call the plumber? The sink's still leaking. You said you'd take care of it last week."

Daniel rubbed his forehead. "I'll get to it."

"You said that before." Rachel stepped into view, spoon in hand, and the baby fussing in the highchair behind her. "And Ethan's preschool forms, I had to do those too. Daniel, you keep saying you'll handle things, but..."

"Okay, enough!" His voice cracked like a whip, harsher than he realized. The baby startled into a wail, face crumpling. His wife's eyes hardened, then dropped. She turned back to the stove, shoulders rigid, without another word.

The silence that followed was worse than an argument would have been.

Daniel sank into a chair, elbows on knees, staring at one end of the kitchen table. His kids were at the other end. It felt like they were miles away. Guilt hit instantly, like a punch to the gut. He hadn't meant to snap. He never meant to snap. But lately, the smallest things tipped him over the edge.

That's when the Critic arrived, swift and merciless.

"You just left work while everyone else is still there, making an impression.

And for what purpose? To just explode for no reason, so I guess you're failing here, too.

She doesn't believe you'll follow through. And she's right. You're stretched too thin. You're not the husband she needs. Not the man you promised you'd be.

But I guess that is par for the course because you aren't exactly killing it at work either these days."

The words were not shouted, but they pressed hard, and they were suffocating.

His phone buzzed on the counter. Another work email. He didn't check it. What was the point? One more fire waiting to be put out. One more reminder that no matter how hard he ran, the world was always three steps ahead.

"Daddy?" A small voice tugged him out of his haze.

Daniel looked up. Ethan was staring at him from the table, clutching a toy truck to his chest. "Play with me?"

Daniel's jaw clenched. The timing couldn't be worse. "Not now, buddy."

Ethan hesitated, then jumped down from the table and stepped to where Daniel was sitting, tugging his sleeve gently. "Please?"

"I said not now!" Daniel barked.

The boy flinched, eyes wide. He dropped the truck, the plastic clattering against the hardwood, and bolted down the hall. A door slammed shut.

The sound of the slamming door pulled Daniel backward in time. For a moment, it wasn't Ethan running down the hall; it was him. Seven years old, clutching a baseball glove too big for his hand, standing in the kitchen doorway of his own childhood home.

His father had just gotten home, briefcase still in hand, tie loosened from a long day. Daniel had asked timidly, "Will you play catch with me, Dad?"

The reply was sharp and impatient. "Not now. I'm tired. Go outside by yourself."

The sting of rejection had burned then, but what cut deeper was the pattern. Repeatedly, he learned the same lesson: Daddy's busy, you need to wait until later. In his experience, later rarely arrived, and a dad's world was too full for your small requests. He learned it was best not to ask too much from others. Daniel also learned that people grow up and join a race that seems to make them anything but happy. And apparently winning at life requires certain sacrifices, but it was worth it in the end because... That was the part of the lesson that was never clear: What exactly did all this winning add up to?

Now, decades later, Daniel heard his own voice, an echo of his father's. It was harsh, clipped, and rejecting. It was hurled at his little boy. The echo was unmistakable. The boy he had been, and the boy he was raising, both wounded by the same two words: Not now.

A sick dread settled in his chest. He had sworn he would be different, that Ethan would never have to wonder if his dad wanted him around. Yet here he was, carrying forward the very wound he once hated.

The Critic pounced on the opening. *"You see? You're no better than him. You thought you could be different, but you're not. You're just another man who strives but delivers the same disappointment. He'll grow up remembering the slam of your voice, not the warmth of your presence."*

The sound echoed through Daniel's chest. He closed his eyes, feeling the searing hot shame.

"Now you've done it- First your wife, now your kid. They'll remember this. The yelling, the distance, not the times you tried. You're weak. You're stretched thin. And it's never enough."

His pulse quickened, thoughts spiraling. He pictured Mark out there winning: He had new deals while traveling to new cities, and he was living big. Mark was confident, polished, and untouchable. And here he was, snapping at a four-year-old.

The Critic chimed in, *"You don't measure up. You never will."*

The spiral tightened. Every thought darker than the last. His chest ached, shallow breaths catching like he was underwater. He pressed his palms hard against his eyes, desperate to block it all out, to stop the reel from spinning.

Somewhere in the house, the baby's cries continued, his wife moving back and forth with hurried footsteps. The sound of water boiling over hissed from the stove. The ordinary chaos of home, but to Daniel, it felt unbearable, deafening.

He couldn't shake the image of Ethan's face when he yelled. The way the boy recoiled, not just from the sound, but from him. His own son had looked at him with fear. That cut deeper than any words his wife could throw at him.

The shame was heavy. Crushing.

His phone buzzed again. He nearly ignored it; he just couldn't face another reminder of everything he hadn't done. But the screen lit up with a name that was not from work.

John.

"Good to meet the other day. I'd like to continue our conversation. How about coffee later this week?"

Daniel blinked at the message. He read it once. Twice. A third time.

The storm in his head didn't vanish, but it slowed just slightly. The Critic's voice dulled, pushed back by something gentler. Someone thought he was worth another conversation. Someone believed there was still something worth investing in him.

He let out a shaky breath. The kitchen noises carried on, the baby still fussing, his wife still silent, the sink still leaking. Nothing outside had changed.

But inside, something cracked open — not in collapse, but in release.

For the first time all evening, a flicker of hope stirred.

Maybe he didn't have to figure this out alone.

Daniel stood slowly, the weight still there but no longer crushing. He bent down, picked up the little red truck from where it lay abandoned on the floor. He turned it over in his hands, thumb tracing the chipped paint. Then he walked down the hall, pausing at the closed door.

He knocked gently.

"Hey, buddy," he said softly, voice catching. "I'm sorry. Can I come in?"

There was no reply, just the muffled quiet of a boy hiding. Daniel leaned his forehead against the door, the toy still in his hand.

"I'll try again later," he whispered, more to himself than to Ethan.

And at that moment, he believed he actually would.

6

Warming Up To Learning A New Way To Run

The men's group had thinned out for the night. Folding chairs scraped and echoed across the fellowship hall floor, the sound bouncing off cinder block walls that had hosted countless late-night conversations like the one that just ended. The smell of coffee lingered, burnt slightly from the metal carafe that had been reheated one too many times.

Paul lingered near the back, nursing the last swallow from his Styrofoam cup. Across the room, John gathered his notes into a neat stack. On the surface, he was finished for the night. But his eyes were distant, his movements slower than usual, like a man carrying something unseen.

Paul caught it instantly. He'd known John too long to miss the signs.

"You're thinking about Daniel, aren't you?"

John looked up, a small half-smile tugging at the corner of his mouth. "I sent him a message earlier this week. Just a simple invitation." He slid the papers into his worn leather folder and snapped it shut. "Haven't heard back yet, but I could tell when we talked the first time, he's carrying more than he knows how to handle."

Paul set the cup aside and leaned forward, elbows on his knees. His voice dropped, the way men talk when the subject is heavy. "He is. Look, Daniel's a good man. Loves his wife, loves those kids. But he's restless. Always has been. He pushes hard because he feels like he has to prove himself to his boss, his wife, his team, maybe even to himself."

John stayed quiet, letting the words hang. He remembered that hunger well: Prove. Perform. Push. It nearly cost him everything.

Paul exhaled. "And his company? Brutal. Cutthroat. Everyone is climbing over each other. He thinks it's too toxic for him to make a difference, so he just tries to survive it. And somewhere along the way, he bought the lie that being a good dad is about making more money, not being more present." He shook his head. "His wife's strong, she keeps things moving at home, but Daniel? He's drowning in angst. And it's eating at him, but he probably doesn't even know that is what makes everything, even winning, feel so empty and lonely."

John folded his hands, voice low but firm. "Provision without presence feels like absence, no matter how much you can provide. I learned that the hard way."

Paul nodded, eyes narrowing as if the phrase had cut through the noise. "That's exactly why I told him to sit down with you. You helped me when I was at the end of my rope. I figure if you could help me, you can help him."

John let the words settle, but his mind was already walking backward in time. To his own breaking point. To the employee survey that exposed his blind spots. To Stan's blunt confrontation. And worst of all, his wife's quiet disappointment, across the dinner table, the look that said she wasn't sure if she could keep believing his promises.

Those scars hadn't faded; they had only hardened into reminders. He thought to himself, "This is what happens when you win using unsustainable methods at work, and so you start to lose everywhere else." He had nearly lost her trust completely, and for years afterward, he had to rebuild it piece by piece.

He could see Daniel in all of it: Young, successful, but still desperately chasing more, and confident he wanted to win in every aspect of life, but uncertain what that actually looked like.

"He doesn't see it yet," John said slowly, choosing his words with care. "But the cracks are already showing. And sometimes… sometimes that's the only way the light gets in."

Paul smirked, but his eyes betrayed the worry beneath. "So, what is your plan? Where do you even start with someone like Daniel?"

John leaned back, folding his arms, gazing steadily and unhurried. "Not with tactics. Not with easy advice. Not even with well-intentioned, feel-good habits like generosity or kindness." He paused, letting the weight of his next words land. "You must start at the core with integrity. Because if you don't put that first, everything else eventually falls apart."

Paul sat back, letting that sink in. The room had gone quiet now, only the hum of the fluorescent lights above them.

John glanced at his folder, then back at Paul. His voice softened. "If Daniel shows up, I'll be ready. But he has to want it. My job is just to open the door, not push him through it."

7

A Break in the Waves

The buzz of his phone shattered the fragile peace in that moment while Daniel was standing in the hallway, considering whether he really had the energy to engage with his son's evening routine.

It was a text from Mark.

Daniel opened the message. A photo filled the screen: Mark, grinning in a tailored suit, stepping into a private jet with champagne in hand and his sunglasses reflecting the Mediterranean sky. The text read: "Headed to Monaco. Client dinner on the yacht tonight. Work hard, play harder. Someday you can get here too, just keep grinding."

Heat surged in Daniel's chest. Of course, Mark was out there living big. He'd figured it out.

The image dragged Daniel back in time. Senior year of college. Business Capstone class. Their professor had assigned a semester-long consulting project with a local company to solve their real-world problem with a real-world solution and a presentation to their board. Daniel remembered the late nights in the library, drafting the research, building the deck, and carrying the weight of the whole project.

Mark breezed in at the end, crisp suit, big smile, charm turned up to full volume. When the client praised the recommendations, Mark was the one who stepped forward, fielding questions, claiming credit, and painting himself as the mastermind. Daniel stood there, exhausted and invisible, while Mark soaked up the applause.

He still remembers his inner Critic telling him, *"Exactly. You're the workhorse, not the winner. Nobody remembers the one in the background."*

The worst part wasn't what happened at the presentation. It was what happened afterwards. Weeks later, the same client invited Mark to a networking dinner. That dinner opened the door to his first consulting job, the launchpad for the flashy career he still flaunts today.

Daniel hadn't kept quiet back then. He remembered pulling Mark aside in the dorm lounge, frustration spilling out.

"Hey, man, that wasn't right. You know I carried the load. You didn't even give me a nod."

Mark smiled, as smoothly as ever, and slung an arm around Daniel's shoulder.

"Danny, relax. That's how the game is played. You did the work; I did the talking, win-win. You'll get your shot. Don't sweat it. Look at the grade we got. We crushed it."

Those words echoed now, years later, as Daniel looked at the photo of Mark by the jet. "That's how the game is played... You'll get your shot..." The inner Critic from back then might have been right. *"See? That's what happens when you don't know how to play the game. You grind; they shine."*

Daniel's jaw tightened. Maybe Mark was right. Maybe all these years he'd been the fool, grinding, waiting for "his shot" that never seemed to come.

By midweek, the illusion of winning cracked again.

Tuesday, Daniel was praised for closing a big deal. His team had worked all night, almost 24 hours straight. There were some big contributions from others, including his protégé Kara, which really helped impress the client. Kara was exceptional at anticipating client needs, and she had identified key inclusions that helped seal the deal. The client concluded that Daniel's team was the perfect fit for delivering just what they needed. It worked, and they closed a deal that some said could not be closed.

Daniel recalls sending the email to the Executive Leadership team when the client confirmed they would sign. He mentioned the efforts of the team, even if he didn't use their specific names, so everyone would get credit. But

Daniel wanted to make sure the leaders recognized that he was the captain of the ship, so he included more details about his heroics instead.

The leaders ate it up, and in the staff meeting on Wednesday, when they announced the big win, Daniel was mentioned by name, but that was it; there was no mention of the rest of the team. His boss went so far as to say in front of everyone that this was exactly why they promoted Daniel so quickly. The leaders said he just knows how to get the right things done to cross the finish line before others even get off the starting line.

Later that day at Daniel's team meeting, the atmosphere felt a little off. Daniel couldn't understand why it wasn't filled with joy and high fives with the team having just been recognized for the big win. It just didn't make sense. Clearly, everyone knew Daniel couldn't have done it all on his own; it's not his fault that the culture only recognizes the guy at the top.

Daniel had worked hard to get to the top, and he deserved to be recognized after years in the shadows. The Critic was quick to add more support to his argument.

"You deserve the credit; it's about time someone noticed your great leadership. You really nailed it. You are a great asset, and the only mistake was in how long it took you to get promoted."

The Critic encouraged Daniel to dismiss his team's lack of enthusiasm for the win as jealousy. They were just not seeing the big picture that when Daniel wins, the team wins. It is all the same; it's just schematics whose names get shared.

He closed the team meeting quickly; he didn't want anyone to cast a shadow over what should have been a big celebration.

As he left the conference room, Kara was waiting for him in the hall.

"Daniel, you know the team worked just as hard as you did; in fact, a couple of team members missed their kids' school events to make sure we got the win." Her tone was more direct than he was used to, and frankly, he didn't appreciate it, not because she was wrong, but because she was right.

"Kara, no one thinks I did all the work myself; that is ridiculous. It's just the way we do things here. We recognize the person at the top for ease, and they make sure the team knows they are also appreciated."

Kara wasn't emotional; she was resolved. This wasn't the first time she'd seen the team overlooked, and she wasn't going to ignore it again. "Daniel, that is just not okay. It really hurts us that you don't seem to care how we feel or what we experience working under you. We may be a team in name, but it feels like we are a bunch of individuals who report to you."

Kara stormed off before Daniel could reply.

Daniel knew that Kara had a gift for reading people and anticipating relational cracks long before he did. She was often able to help the team proactively avoid disaster, and he appreciated it greatly, although he never acknowledged any of this to her.

Before Daniel seriously considered Kara's insights and accusations, the Critic went back on the offensive. *"See, Daniel, Kara is jealous. Are you sure she is the right person to be your second-in-command? You would never talk to your boss like that. That is not how you get ahead in this company."*

Daniel was content with the Critic's reasoning; it was good to have him on his side.

Daniel sent Mark a reply to his earlier text. "Hey, I know it isn't Dubai, but I just closed a huge deal. Getting closer to the BIG PAY days you are always talking about. Work hard. Play hard."

He hit send and saw that Mark received and immediately read the text, but no bubbles popped up to indicate a reply was coming his way. He was a bit taken aback but just chalked it up to Mark being in the middle of closing his own "big" deal. That is just how the big timers do it.

By the time Daniel was driving home, the Critic's mantra had hardened: *"You are the man. You ran faster, harder, and longer than everyone else. You deserve the credit and are ready for even more. If the team knows what is good for them, they will just stay on the Daniel rocket all the way to the top."*

Daniel was looking forward to getting home to tell Rachel the good news about how he was killing it at work. The driveway light flickered on automatically as Daniel pulled in. He barely let the engine die before he jumped out of the car and sprinted towards the door.

He pushed the door open with a smile on his face, ready to share the good news. But before he could even get a word out, Rachel called from the kitchen.

"Did you call the insurance company like I asked?" His wife's voice was not angry, just tired.

Daniel froze. He had forgotten. Again.

"I'll do it tomorrow," he muttered, pulling at his tie.

"Tomorrow?" She stepped into view, with the dish towel over her shoulder, and her eyes narrowing just slightly. "Daniel, they have been waiting for the paperwork for two weeks. If you don't—"

"I said I'll do it!" His voice came out sharper than he meant, but once it was out, he couldn't pull it back.

She blinked, caught off guard. "I'm just trying to—"

"To what? Remind me of all the ways I'm failing? Do you think I just didn't do it because I don't care? I was busy closing a huge deal at work. It is the kind of deal the bosses finally recognized and shared with everyone how much I mean to the company, how they are glad they promoted me."

Daniel continued, "Did it occur to you that maybe I didn't do it because other important things are happening in my life? That I was focused on something that matters to me and will actually improve our lives, too?"

Her lips parted, but she didn't answer. That silence was worse than words. It landed heavy, like confirmation he was in this race alone.

"Daddy?" A small voice cut through the haze.

His daughter stood at the bottom of the stairs, holding a toy with one arm dangling loose. "Can you fix it?"

The plastic was cracked, and the paint was peeling. She looked up at him, eyes wide with hope.

And Daniel snapped.

"Not now!" His shout filled the room. The little girl flinched, her bottom lip trembling. "Can't you see I just walked in the door and your mom has already reminded me of something I forgot to do? Can't I get just one minute of peace?"

Her eyes filled with tears, and she turned, running into the open arms of her mother. Tiny whimpers muffled in the fabric of Rachel's sweatshirt. Those muffled tears still managed to sound like bullhorns.

Daniel left the kitchen and headed for the couch. He sank into it, head in his hands. His chest ached, his temples pounded. He could still hear the echo of his own voice, harsh and jagged. He pictured his daughter's face — startled, hurt — and the weight of shame pressed down harder.

The events of the day layered together into a single chorus: He is a winner at work, but that comes at a cost at home. And sometimes that cost is collateral damage; he can make it better tomorrow, but today he is going to celebrate his win even if he has to celebrate alone.

From inside his pocket, his phone buzzed. He pulled it out and took a look, hoping it was Mark; someone was going to join Daniel's celebration.

It wasn't Mark.

It was John.

"Hey Daniel, just wanted to pass this along: Remember, we aren't made for isolation; we are made for community. I would really love to talk more soon. Coffee is on me. Hope you had a great day."

Daniel stared at the message. Direct. Almost annoyingly simple. And yet it pierced through the noise like nothing else had all week.

He had a big win, but his work team didn't react the way he thought they should, and neither did his home team, his family, the ones he works so hard to win for. Come to think of it, he was celebrating alone on the couch while Mark was celebrating with champagne on a yacht.

He didn't reply. He couldn't because he wasn't sure what to even say. But one contradiction bounced around in his mind.

"Two voices. Two visions of life.

One was flashy, loud, and relentless.

The other was steady, quiet, and stubbornly hopeful.

They can't both be right; two things that seem so significantly different can't possibly lead to winning, can they?"

And Daniel sat there, torn between them.

But the contrast lodged deep inside him — one voice pulling him toward the grind, the other toward something he couldn't quite name.

The grinder, Mark, knew Daniel had a big win, and yet didn't give him the time of day with a reply. But John had no idea what kind of day Daniel was having, yet he reached out almost randomly just to offer encouragement and support.

Daniel didn't know what it meant, but John's text definitely felt good, even though it didn't mention the big win. It might have even felt better than the win at work, but that couldn't be possible, could it?

8

The Final Breaking Point

The next morning, Daniel shuffled downstairs, half-dressed, hair still wet from the shower. The kitchen was a swirl of chaos — cereal bowls and spoons clattering, one child searching for a missing shoe, another tugging on their mother's sleeve. Baby in the highchair, picking at Cheerios.

His wife stood at the stove, spatula in hand, shoulders stiff. She didn't look up as he entered.

"Morning," he tried, sliding a hand along the counter.

She exhaled sharply. "Morning."

He poured himself coffee, tried to act casual, but the silence pressed in. Finally, she set the spatula down and turned toward him. Her eyes looked tired, and her voice was trembling just enough to make it clear how close she was to the edge.

"Daniel, I can't do this anymore. I feel like a single parent most days. You're either at work, thinking about work, or recovering from work. When you are around it's like your body is present, but your attention is everywhere else."

He swallowed hard. "I'm doing the best I can."

Her voice cracked. "But your 'best' feels like it's killing us. I just... I'm not sure this is what I bargained for."

The words landed like stones in his chest. He wanted to defend himself, to explain how the pressure was suffocating him, too, but the look on her face stopped him. He couldn't respond at all.

Daniel walked back upstairs, as his wife's words echoed behind him like a bell that wouldn't stop ringing: "I just... I'm not sure this is what I bargained for."

He slammed the bedroom door, feeling frustrated and misunderstood. *"Not what you signed up for? Are you kidding me?"* The Critic's voice was already roaring. *"You're out there every single day grinding, with long hours and endless meetings, dragging yourself home with nothing left in the tank, so others don't have to worry about the race. You're doing your best to provide for every one of their needs."*

He tugged at a shirt on a hanger, the fabric nearly tearing in his grip. The Critic went on, *"She wants to talk about signing up? Did you sign up to get flak from your team at work? To bust your tail for scraps while Mark gets further ahead? Does she think you enjoy missing your family events, walking in when dinner's cold, or seeing that look in her eyes?"*

The Critic pushed harder, circling him like a boxer in the ring.

"Face it, Daniel: You're failing. Even when you win, you lose. Everyone's passing you: Mark, with his picture-perfect life. And your team is trying to sabotage you so they can climb over you. Even your wife is doubting if you're enough."

He shook his head violently, yanking a pair of pants off the chair. He thought to himself, "No. I'm carrying it all. Without me, this house falls apart, the team returns to being average, and the company loses its best clients. If I don't keep grinding, if I don't keep pushing, who's going to do it? Nobody. It's got to be me. I will carry the load."

He jammed his hand into the pocket, muttering under his breath. His fingers brushed on paper. "What the..." He pulled out a folded note, his heart still pounding.

Paul's handwriting.

He sat down heavily on the bed, still fuming, and opened it.

"Daniel, you once told me, 'I feel like I'm always running and everyone else is passing me by.' I said that exact same thing once. John was the one who helped me through it. He showed me I wasn't falling behind; I was just running the race the wrong way, and I needed to adopt a new approach. I think you'd really benefit from meeting him. – Paul"

Daniel froze.

His exact words, the ones that had been bouncing like punches in his skull, even this morning: 'Everyone is passing me by,' stared back at him in ink.

He took a deep breath, anger still simmering, but something cracked open. His Critic went quiet, just for a moment.

He remembered the note. Paul had handed it to Daniel one day in the men's group. It was Paul's reply to a conversation they had over text where Daniel was venting about how he left work early to attend Ethan's preschool play, and in his absence, a client email completely blew up. The team tried to handle it, but they were missing a key piece of information that only Daniel knew, so they actually made things worse. Daniel was sharing with Paul how he felt like he couldn't win; it was always a choice between home and work. He couldn't figure out how to have both, and every time he chose home, it felt like he was failing at work and losing the race.

Then, a thought flashed through Daniel's mind, something he hadn't considered in a long time: "Maybe… Maybe I'm not alone."

For reasons he couldn't explain, Daniel tucked the note back into his pocket and walked into the kitchen. "Hey," he said quietly, softer this time. "Let's sit down and eat together."

His wife blinked, wary, but she sat. For once this morning, Daniel lingered instead of bolting out the door. He cut up the eggs, buttered the toast, and even managed a small laugh at something his son said. It wasn't perfect, nothing close, but it was something. A truce, maybe. A peace offering gesture signaling he knew he was falling short of what was needed from him.

When breakfast was done, he kissed his kids, squeezed his wife's shoulder, and grabbed his keys. As he stepped into the garage, he thought that maybe this was what an apology looked like. Maybe this was a start.

But as he started the car, his phone buzzed. The screen lit with a message from his boss: "Where are you? The client meeting got moved to this morning. I need your input."

The weight crashed back down. Daniel gripped the steering wheel hard, his knuckles white as he whispered under his breath, "I can't take one more thing. Not today."

The phone buzzed again. This time, the screen lit up with a familiar name: John. "Hey, I've got three tickets to the big game this weekend. Want to come with me?"

Daniel froze. The big game. The one everyone in the city had been talking about for months. Tickets were impossible to get.

His Critic tried to pounce. *"Why would he ask you? You barely know him. One coffee conversation and a bunch of unanswered texts, and he is offering you a ticket to THE GAME. There must be a hidden agenda."*

But for once, Daniel didn't argue, didn't over analyze. He just felt the need for a release of pressure from all the meetings, the comparisons, the fight in the kitchen, and the hollow victories. He needed a break from it all.

And before he could talk himself out of it, he grabbed his phone and texted. "Sure, I'd love to go."

He hit send and stared at the screen, the tiniest flicker of something unfamiliar breaking through the haze.

Hope.

9

A New Way to Race Revealed

Daniel sat in the car for a long minute after hitting send.

"Sure, I'd love to go."

He stared at the words, the tiny blue bubble that had left his phone and landed somewhere in John's world. His thumb hovered as if he might pull it back, delete it, undo it somehow. Too late.

Another buzz.

"Great, here's the address. Saturday, 10:30. Tickets are on me, but food's your department."

Daniel exhaled, shaking his head. Who was this guy? Daniel had ignored his last few texts; they only had one hurried coffee, and now he was offering Daniel one of the most coveted tickets in town.

His Critic started circling again. *"You don't deserve this. He probably invited you out of pity. Or worse, he needs something. Nobody gives without an angle."*

He jammed the car into reverse, muttering under his breath. But even as he grumbled, something in him knew the Critic was wrong. John's message hadn't read like pity. It had read like… an invitation.

Saturday at the Big Game

The city pulsed with energy, jerseys everywhere, horns blaring. Daniel parked and started scanning for John. He almost turned around twice and got back in his car. What was he doing here? He didn't belong. He should be at home, catching up on bills, or at the office, working through the stack of reports he hadn't finished.

Then he saw him. John waved, with a broad grin, like they'd known each other for years. Paul was with him, too.

"Daniel! Over here!"

They walked amongst the crowd to the stadium, exchanging small talk along the way.

The seats were close enough to see the sweat on the players. John handed him a program, clapped him on the back, and for a while, Daniel just let himself get lost in the game. Cheering, high-fiving strangers, yelling at refs. Something loosened in his chest that he didn't know he'd been carrying.

At halftime, John leaned closer. "Paul told me a little about what you're going through."

Daniel stiffened. "Oh?"

"Nothing detailed. Just enough to know you've been running hard. Have had a few nice wins, but feeling like you can't keep up."

Daniel looked down at his hands, ready to deflect, but John wasn't pressing. His tone was casual, even kind.

"You know," John said, "a while back I was in the same place. Grinding nonstop. Winning, but somehow always feeling behind. Always second-guessing myself. I thought the only way out of it was to run faster."

Daniel glanced up. John's eyes held no judgment, just quiet recognition.

"What changed?" Daniel asked before he could stop himself.

John leaned toward Daniel with a question that seemed almost out of place.

"Daniel, look around this field… What's on the outside of it?"

Daniel glanced around, unsure. Grass, painted lines, the crowd. Then he noticed what John must have meant: The running track circling the field.

"A track," he muttered, uneasy about where this was headed.

"That's right," John nodded. "I think a track is a perfect metaphor of how most of us live. We've all heard the phrase 'life is a race.' And in a way, that's fair — we each start at the beginning when we're born, and one day there's a finish line. But most of us never stop to question how we're supposed to run it."

He let the thought hang for a moment before pressing further. "Tell me, Daniel, who taught you how to run your race?"

Daniel frowned. He didn't remember anyone ever sitting him down to explain it. So, he said what came naturally, "I guess I just picked it up along the way."

"Exactly," John said. "Most of us learn by watching the people around us. Our families, our peers, our bosses, even our spouses. Nobody hands us a playbook. We just watch others run, then mimic their pace, their posture, their priorities. That's how we figure out the 'rules.'"

Daniel shifted uncomfortably. He wasn't sure he liked where this was going.

John continued anyway. "For me, I learned from my dad: Work harder than everyone else. Don't ask for help. Don't show weakness. Just keep going. I never heard him say those words directly, but I saw them in his late nights at the office, his constant complaints about coworkers, and the way he never apologized. He believed winning meant outlasting everyone else."

Before Daniel could respond, Paul chimed in. "And John will also tell you he is speaking from experience, living that way almost cost him everything. His health, his marriage, even his team at work."

John gave Paul a wry smile. "He's not wrong. I ran hard, and I collected all the medals. But eventually, I realized I wasn't just tired, I was running the race the wrong way. And when I looked for someone who could show me another way, no one had a plan. That was the most hopeless part. I hit the bottom, humbled myself to ask for help, and no one was ready to share a playbook for what running differently actually looked like.

Daniel frowned. "So, you're saying the problem isn't that we're in the wrong race?"

"Exactly," John said. "It's not about quitting. It's not about swearing off ambition or achievement. Winning isn't a bad thing, and I am not saying success needs to be avoided at all costs. The problem is how most of us think we need to run the race to win. When the way we run drains us, isolates us from people in our lives, or leaves us secretly hoping others will fail so we can pull ahead… That's when we need to learn a new way to run."

Paul leaned in again. "That's what John showed me. We don't need to stop running. We need to learn a different stride."

John nodded. "Running differently is what makes winning feel like you have always thought winning would.

When you adjust how you run, your success in one area isn't at the expense of losing somewhere else in your life. Your new pace allows you to run with others instead of against them, so you gain relationships as well.

Daniel sat back, letting it sink in. He could feel the weight of John's words because he recognized the truth in them — the constant sprinting, the endless comparisons, the way his victories left him emptier and more alone than he expected.

John finished with a quiet conviction: "When you learn to run the wiser way, the finish line doesn't always have to change. What changes is how you choose to set and maintain your pace."

John leaned back, watching the players gather on the field. "That's the key, Daniel. The problem isn't that you're in the wrong race, it's that you're running it the wrong way. And if you want to run differently, you need a new playbook."

"A playbook?" Daniel asked, feeling confused.

John nodded. "Yeah. It took me years to figure this out, but over time, I realized seven approaches to running that changed everything. Not theories. Not slogans. But specific intentional mindsets to practice, whether I was in a boardroom, at my dinner table, or coaching Little League. They made running feel better and winning more like what I believed winning was supposed to feel like. I call them the GENUINE advantage."

Daniel's eyes narrowed. "Seven?"

"Yes, think of them like the batons runners pass in a relay race," John said, his voice steady. "You don't win this race by sprinting alone. One of the most important things I learned is that the race isn't a solo sprint; it's a team relay. You win the race by learning how to carry, pass, and receive the right batons with the people around you." He held out his hand and began sharing the batons by counting his fingers, one by one:

- "**Generous**. Not just money. Generous with time, credit, and attention. When you give, people run with you instead of against you.
- **Engaged**. Fully present. Not half in, half out. Engagement is how you show people they matter as you are running the race with them.
- **Nice**. But not generic or soft pleasantries. Kindness that's personal, specific. The gesture that says, 'I see you, and you matter.' That baton gets remembered.
- **Unafraid**. Courage with vulnerability. The guts to run a race others quit at the starting line, but also the humility to admit mistakes, and that you can't do it all alone; you need your team.
- **Integrity**. Running as one whole person. The same stride everywhere you go. No masks. No fractured versions of you. One consistent person running a consistent pace.
- **Non-Judgmental.** Curiosity over Criticism. You don't know the track someone else has been on, but you can learn to run alongside them and pick them up when they stumble instead of running past them.
- **Empathy**. Slowing down enough to feel somcone else's pace, their pain, their perspective. That's how you stop running alone when times are hard."

Daniel sat forward, elbows on his knees. He could hear the crowd, see the players, but his mind was locked on those seven principles, the batons waiting to be passed.

John leaned closer. "Daniel, running differently doesn't mean stopping. It means choosing when to carry the baton on your own and when to pass it off. You don't need to master all seven today. Just pick one. Try it out. At work. At home. Anywhere. You change the way you run by adjusting your approach one step at a time."

Daniel breathed slowly, the list circling in his head. GENUINE. Generous. Engaged. Nice. Unafraid. Integrity. Non-Judgmental. Empathy.

Seven batons. The playbook for running differently sounds like the better way to run the race, the way he should have been running all along.

After the Game

The three of them walked out together, swept along by the crowd. Daniel couldn't shake it. He wanted to ask John more, but he didn't know how to begin.

Paul noticed. "He told you about the race, didn't he?"

Daniel looked over, startled. "The race?"

Paul nodded. "The one you think you have to win alone. The one where you believe if you just push harder, work longer, prove more, then maybe you'll matter. That was me, too."

John smiled faintly but said nothing, letting Paul continue.

"I thought success was about keeping up, outpacing everyone else. But I was running myself into the ground. And then John told me what he just told you, that maybe it wasn't that I was behind, I was just running the race the wrong way."

Paul gave a little smile. "Did John tell you how it's not even about you training to run faster or longer. It blew my mind to consider that life is more like a relay than a solo sprint. That you aren't supposed to carry the whole load on your own. The idea that the race was a team sport never occurred to me. I had always just run as fast as I could. And it honestly made me mad when I realized that winning could be achieved by running my lap, then handing the baton to someone else to run for a bit, so I could catch my breath. But it's true. When you run like a relay, you get twice as far with half the effort. That's a playbook for a sustainable winning pace."

The words rang in Daniel's ears. "A relay. Not a solo sprint." But almost immediately, the Critic appeared with his own advice. *"That's weak. Handing things off means admitting you can't do it. Successful people don't stop or need help. You think Mark slows down? He's miles ahead of you already. You can't afford to pass anything to anyone. If you let go, everything falls apart."*

Daniel tried to force the thoughts away, but they kept circling through his mind.

As they arrived at the parking lot, the stadium lights still glowing behind them, Paul placed a hand on Daniel's shoulder.

"Daniel. You don't need a different race. You need a different way to run it. A pace that's not about proving yourself, but about building something that lasts."

Daniel felt his throat tighten. The exhaustion of the past months, the wins that felt like losses, the slammed bedroom doors, the comparisons with Mark, the fights at home, the Critic's voice — it all pressed in. He didn't know what to say.

But he knew this: For the first time, he was open to considering he wasn't the first to struggle and that maybe he didn't need to struggle alone.

The Napkin Notes

On the drive home, Daniel couldn't shake it. The stadium noise still rang faintly in his ears, but John's words were louder. "Not the wrong race... the wrong way to run."

He pulled into the driveway and sat for a moment in the quiet car. He didn't want the thoughts to get lost, so he grabbed the only thing he could find, a crumpled napkin in his pocket from the concession stand. Leaning it against the steering wheel, he scribbled a few lines, trying to make sense of it all:

It's not about stopping the race. The key is learning to run it the wiser way.

1. We were made to run. Achievement isn't the problem, but the way we chase it might be.
2. Most of us learn how to run by copying others. Family. Friends. Bosses. Spouses. Marketers. We never stop to ask if their way is actually wise.

3. Here's what I learned and maybe got wrong as I started to run:

- I thought it was a solo sprint; only one person got the medal at the end.
- I thought every lap had to be won by as wide a margin as possible. So always sprint longer, harder, further, faster.
- I thought comparing to everyone else was the key — pushing harder if they were close, finding cracks if they were in front, sometimes even rooting for them to fall.
- I measured my life by my house, my car, my financials, and my ability to perform well in front of others.

Maybe I need to use the 7 batons to run differently. What were the batons?

Daniel set the pen down. The words stared back at him, raw and unsettling. He folded the napkin and walked toward the front door.

Whatever conversation was waiting inside, he knew this much: He couldn't keep running the same way. And if he was going to change, it wouldn't just be about his work; it would have to start at home.

Back in the House

The house lights glowed softly as Daniel opened the door. The smell of dinner lingered in the air, but the plates were already cleared. Rachel was at the sink, sleeves rolled up, and the quiet scrape of silverware against a dish was the only sound in the room.

Daniel slipped the folded napkin into his pocket before she could see it. He didn't even know how to explain it yet.

"You're late," Rachel said without turning around. Her voice wasn't sharp, just tired.

"I know." He hesitated, searching for words. "I, uh… stayed to chat after the game."

She looked over her shoulder, surprised. "Chat? Who did you stay to chat with?"

"John and Paul. John is the guy Paul introduced me to, who invited me to the game." He leaned his elbows on the table. "It's strange... John barely knows me, but he keeps showing up. He's... generous. He listens, actually listens. He doesn't rush in with advice, and he doesn't make me feel small. He's present in a way I can't remember the last time I was. He's not trying to impress anyone, not trying to judge me. He's just... real. And for those few hours, I wasn't performing. I wasn't defending myself or trying to prove something. I was just there enjoying other people."

Rachel dried her hands and leaned against the counter, studying him. "And how was that?"

Daniel exhaled, "Different. We talked about... well, about life. About how maybe it's not that I'm in the wrong race, but maybe I've just been running the race of life the wrong way."

Her eyes softened with curiosity. "And what does the 'right way' look like?"

He shook his head, a faint smile tugging at the corner of his mouth. "I don't know yet. But maybe it's time to find out if there really is a different way to run."

Rachel didn't say anything right away. She just held his gaze, then her eyes welled, and she whispered, "Daniel, I don't need you to always win. I just need you to let me run the race with you."

The Critic pounced again. "What? She thinks it's not about winning. Well, how is she going to feel if you start losing? Does she really want to run with you? Didn't she just say she wasn't even sure she wanted to run together anymore, and questioned if this was what she bargained for?"

Daniel wanted to remind her of her words and question if she really meant it, but then he remembered non-judgmental was one of the batons, and so he chose to remain quiet. Instead of picking a battle, he picked up her hand and just held it.

10

Sunday Morning Drive

The next morning felt… lighter. Just a little. Daniel came downstairs dressed neatly, not feeling rushed, his hair still intentionally messy after his shower. He set his phone on the counter instead of scrolling while he sipped his coffee. His wife noticed, brow raised as she turned her gaze from her own cell phone and looked at him.

"You're… different this morning," she said carefully.

Daniel shrugged. "Trying to run differently."

She hesitated. "Would you come with us to church today?"

In this moment, he didn't flinch. "Yeah. Sure. I think I will."

Her eyes softened, surprised but hopeful. The kids noticed, too, their chatter bubbling at the thought of Dad joining them.

The drive was noisy at first with the music playing and the kids squabbling, but somewhere along the route, silence crept in, and Daniel's thoughts drifted.

A billboard for a new luxury car slid past, its glossy sheen catching his eye. Immediately, the inner Critic surged. *"You should have one of those by now."*

It wasn't just a whisper this time. The Critic slid into the back middle seat, wearing a sharp suit with his hair slicked back. His smile was cold, his timing calculating.

"You're falling behind, Daniel. Remember Mark? Do you think he is taking it easy this morning? Is that going to score you a bigger house or better numbers?

45

How does sitting in traffic or eating breakfast with the kids make up for your mediocrity or help you win?"

Daniel gripped the wheel. He could feel the energy draining, the fragile peace from that morning slipping.

Then he paused, took a deep breath, and thought to himself, "What would John do right now?"

The Critic scoffed, straightening his cuff links. *"John? Please. He's not the measure. You're in a race, Daniel. And you're losing. Don't you see? That's why you're miserable. You are miserable because you know you can run harder. More deals, more hours, more status. If you don't pick up the pace, you'll never catch up. Everyone else is sprinting while you're stuck in place."*

Then, suddenly, Daniel realized that the Critic wasn't just urging him to win; he was chaining him to a pace that could never be sustained. Endless laps. No finish line. No relay, no teammates, just exhaustion. And the ones left staring from the sidelines — his wife, his kids, even part of himself — were the ones paying for his sprinter's pace.

His lungs felt heavy at the thought, as if he were already out of breath, chasing a finish line that would never come. He exhaled slowly. His grip loosened on the wheel.

In his mind, another picture flickered with the images of John, who is steady and generous, offering his tickets and time. And Paul, who is patient and non-judgmental as he waits for Daniel to catch on. And his wife, asking persistently for him to engage instead of constantly being accusatory.

The Critic is constant and loud, but maybe he's wrong. Maybe he's actually the enemy who's been driving his thoughts and his life for too long.

He didn't say it out loud. Not yet. But Daniel was beginning to believe there was a choice: Keep sprinting alone for a finish line that always seemed to be moving, or change the perspective long enough to figure out if there really was a different way to run the race.

He thought about John and how his pace seemed to be different. Daniel didn't know too much about him, but John's stride seemed… more measured. He wasn't sprinting past people. He was running alongside them. And somehow, he didn't look like he was losing. And being around him felt really good.

A Different Kind of Pace

The Church service let out under a bright autumn sun, and the kids were racing toward the playground while parents clustered in small circles of conversation. Daniel lingered by the steps, with his hands in his pockets. He felt… off-balance. Not in a bad way, but more like he was trying to get his bearings even though he was on a path he'd taken a hundred times before.

John and Paul spotted him before he could slip away. John's grin carried the same ease as it had at the game. Paul gave a nod, steady as ever.

"Glad you came," Paul said with a smile.

Daniel shrugged. "Didn't want to spend another morning running." The words were out before he realized how true they were.

John tilted his head. "Running where?"

Daniel hesitated, then chuckled uncomfortably. "That's the problem. It feels like an uncertain finish line. Or maybe just in… circles."

John didn't fill the silence. He let it breathe. That was different, too. Most people rushed in to fix, to solve. John just stood there, present, as if the pause itself had value.

Finally, John spoke. "You ever watch a relay? Not the speed of the runners, but the exchange of the baton?"

Daniel looked confused, unsure. John went on.

"It's the strangest thing. It doesn't matter how fast you are if you fumble the handoff. A race can be won or lost in the way you pass the baton just as much as in the speed at which you run. Relay runners spend as much time practicing the pass as they do running down the track."

Daniel got lost in his thoughts. His mind flashed back to the Critic, sharp suit and sharper tongue, telling him to grind for more. More hours. More wins. More status. But John was painting another picture: Not a lonely sprint, but something connected, something about pace, presence, and passing things along.

He didn't answer John. He couldn't just yet. But as his kids tugged at his sleeve while joyfully laughing, he felt another crack in the Critic's certainty. Maybe there was another way to run the race that still led to winning.

At Home – Small Cracks, Small Shifts

Dinner that night felt different, and Daniel wasn't sure why. Maybe it was the sermon still echoing faintly in his head. Or maybe it was the way John had talked about the relay, and the idea that sprinting alone wasn't required for winning.

His wife set down a bowl of salad. Normally, she'd eat standing at the counter while cleaning and multitasking, moving faster than anyone else in the house. Daniel would sit scrolling on his phone endlessly. But tonight, she sat at the table, and Daniel's phone remained on the counter. She looked across at him, eyebrows lifted, as if waiting for him to retrieve his phone or excuse himself to go to the office.

But Daniel stayed present. He asked his son about T-ball, and he actually listened to the answer. He noticed his daughter rolling her eyes at him because Daniel tried to tell a bad joke. When the baby flipped his bowl onto the kitchen floor, he laughed out loud instead of fuming over the mess it had just made.

His wife tilted her head and looked at Daniel. "Are you okay? You are really acting strange."

Daniel hesitated. He looked around the table at his home team. "I am great. Just trying to move at a different pace tonight."

For the first time in months, her shoulders softened, she smiled warmly, and said nothing. And for the first time in years, Daniel didn't feel the need to fill the silence.

At Work – The Critic Returns

Monday morning, the office buzzed with the false urgency Daniel thrives on. Emails marked "urgent." Instant Messages pinging. A client pacing the hallway.

The Critic was there, of course, lounging against the glass wall of Daniel's office. Suit crisp, and his smirk was sharper than ever.

"See?" the Critic whispered. *"This is where you shine. Forget breakfast tables and preparing for fake relays. This is the real race, and you are a champion."*

Daniel sat at his desk, staring at the flood of messages. For a moment, he almost believed it. Almost.

Then he remembered John, not his words, but his presence. The calmness. The steadiness. The way he didn't rush to fix everything.

Daniel did something small. He closed his laptop for sixty seconds. Just one minute. He walked out into the hall and asked his assistant if she'd eaten breakfast yet. The surprise on her face told him everything. It was clearly the first time anyone had ever asked.

The Critic scoffed. *"This isn't winning. This is taking a break."*

But Daniel noticed something else: The assistant's posture straightening, and the flicker of gratitude in her eyes when she said she had and thanked him for asking. It was small. But it was real.

And Daniel had a fleeting thought: What if having margin in your calendar might be more sustainable than trying to cram in more?

The Ache of Alignment

Later that night, after the kids had gone to bed, Daniel lingered in the hallway outside his daughter's room. He listened to the slow, steady rhythm of breathing through the door — a sound that should have brought peace but instead pressed on him like a weight.

He thought about the version of himself at work: A sharp, driven, and always posturing professional. He thought about the version his wife saw: A distant, irritable, and often exhausted husband. And then the version his kids got: A distracted, half-present dad always glancing at his phone even in the middle of their play time.

"How many Daniels am I, really?" He asked himself.

The question caught him off guard. He leaned against the doorframe, staring at the grain of the wood as if it might hold the answer.

A memory surfaced of a conversation with Paul months ago, back when they used to grab lunch together more often. Paul had said something simple: "The way you show up at work, at home, and with your friends… It's all connected. People can tell when it's the same person and when it's not."

Back then, Daniel had brushed it off, telling himself that compartmental-izing was just what ambitious people did. But tonight, it hit differently.

What if there weren't supposed to be multiple versions of him? What if the strongest life was the one where he didn't have to switch masks depending on the room he was in?

He stood there in the quiet, letting the possibility sting. Until he found a way to live from the same core person within, no matter where he was, who he was with, or what he was doing, he might never feel whole.

The next morning, Daniel woke up to a text notification. It was John.

"I know you're running your race hard, but do you have time for a pit stop this week? We can meet up on Tuesday morning at the same coffee spot where we first met."

Daniel stared at the message longer than he needed to. No lecture. No pressure. Just an invitation, simple and disarming.

He didn't overthink it this time. His fingers tapped the reply almost automatically.

"7:30. See you there."

11

Beginning to Run Differently

Tuesday Morning – The Coffee Shop

The highway was already buzzing. Daniel's hands tapped impatiently on the wheel as he checked the clock on the dashboard. He should have been on his way into the office by now. The deal he'd been working on had a follow-up call later this morning. The Critic slid into the seat beside him, smoother than ever.

"There it is again, more wasted time," the Critic sneered, brushing an imaginary speck of lint off his cuff. *"You could be at your desk, firing off emails, getting ahead, waving at the slackers who show up after you. Instead, you're chasing some feel-good coffee date. Do you really think that's going to move the needle? You're slipping, Daniel. Falling behind."*

Daniel clenched his jaw. He pressed the accelerator a little harder than necessary, as if speed itself could drown the voice out.

"You know what happens when you're not first in? Someone else takes the edge. More deals, more hours, more ground gained while you sit in a café playing student to a man who doesn't even run your race. Pathetic."

The words landed heavily. Daniel felt the ache in his head. By the time he pulled into the parking lot of the coffee shop, doubt was already gnawing at him. Maybe he should just turn around, head to the office, and call it a morning.

He checked his phone. A new message blinked on the screen from John. "Sorry, I'm running a few minutes late. Grab a table, I'll be right there."

The Critic chuckled darkly from the passenger seat. *"Perfect. He's not even here. Look at you waiting around while real players are already hours into their day. You're wasting time, Daniel. You're throwing it away."*

For a moment, Daniel almost believed it. His hand hovered near the gear shift, ready to back out and leave for the office.

Then he paused. He remembered the comfort of Sunday's deep breath of relaxation at home with his family. He pondered John's non-critical persistence in wanting to make time to get to know Daniel, but on Daniel's timeline, not his own. These moments weren't part of his typical playbook, but they felt like a more natural pace.

Daniel turned off the ignition. He sat for a moment, the hum of the engine fading, the weight of the Critic pressing down. Then, slowly, he opened the door and walked toward the café.

Inside, the air smelled of roasted beans and warm pastries. He slid into a corner booth, still unsettled, still battling. But for some reason, he stayed.

Daniel sipped on his coffee and waited for nearly ten minutes before the door opened, and John came in, moving quickly but not frantically. He carried a calmness that seemed out of place in the rush of people grabbing lattes on their way to work.

"Sorry to keep you waiting," John said as he slid into the booth across from Daniel. "One of my neighbors had car trouble on the school run this morning. I couldn't just leave her stranded with kids in the backseat. Got them sorted and then came straight here."

Daniel blinked. The Critic, still whispering in the corner of his mind, scoffed. *"See? Already wasting your time. This man's busy fixing strangers' problems while you're losing minutes you'll never get back."*

But something in John's tone cut through the noise. There was no apology laced with self-importance, no story spun to make him look heroic. Just a matter-of-fact explanation. He'd helped because that's what he did.

Daniel nodded, shifting in his seat. "I would've just called a tow truck."

John smiled. "Sometimes showing up matters more than outsourcing."

The words landed heavier than Daniel expected. He stirred his coffee, uneasy, before blurting out: "I don't get it. How do you... not feel like you're falling behind when you do things like that?"

John leaned back. He didn't answer right away, which only made Daniel more aware of how quickly he usually filled silences. Finally, John smiled, "Falling behind... oh yes, still figuring out if you want to embrace a different way to run?"

Daniel shifted in his seat, his hand brushing against his coat pocket. He hesitated, then pulled out the napkin he had scribbled on in his driveway after the game.

"I actually wrote something down after the game," he said quietly, tossing it onto the table. The creases were bent from being carried, the ink slightly smudged.

John raised his eyebrows but stayed silent.

Daniel unfolded it, summarizing his scribbles in a low voice.

"We were made to run. Achievement is okay. Most of us learn by copying others and never ask if what we learned was wise. We run it as a solo sprint. We run like we need to win every lap. I thought I needed to watch others so I could adjust my race based on theirs, even hoping for them to fail so I could pass them. I measure life by my house, car, and financials."

His throat tightened. "And... I didn't write this down, but I think I am picking up that there isn't a variety of different races where we need to change how we run; it's just one race, and we can use the same approach to run our race all the time."

Then he finished, "Plus, you mentioned seven habits, I think you called them batons, but frankly, I couldn't remember all of them."

The words hung between them.

John tapped the napkin gently. "That napkin matters. You remembered some important points we talked about and honestly shared your own experience in running the race as well. But the ways you run the race today aren't absolute truths. They are your perceptions based on a variety of things, including what you picked up by watching others run."

Daniel looked down, silent.

"Carrying those assumptions," John said softly, "is like running with weights on your legs. You're moving, but the race feels heavier than it should be, than it can be. You feel slowed down, never free to hit your natural stride or enter your peak performance zone."

He tapped the edge of the napkin. "See, some people feel the weight and think they need to find a new race. So, they go looking for a new track, like a new job, new relationships, or a hobby. But they bring the same approach to running that new race, and soon enough, they find out that the way they run feels just as heavy and limiting there, too."

John continued, "The secret to feeling free while you run isn't found in adjusting the finish line or picking a new track; it's in learning a new way to run the race. And to do that, you need a playbook that helps you tell the lies apart from the truth."

Daniel folded the napkin again, covering it with his hand, not quite ready to put it away.

John reached for a clean napkin from the basket and pulled a pen from his pocket. He unfolded it into two halves, steady and deliberate. "Let's start writing you a new napkin, a new playbook. Here's how I started."

He sketched three columns on the napkin:

- What the Voice Says I Need to Do (How I run)
- What I get from it (What I win)
- What It's Costing Me (What weights I carry)

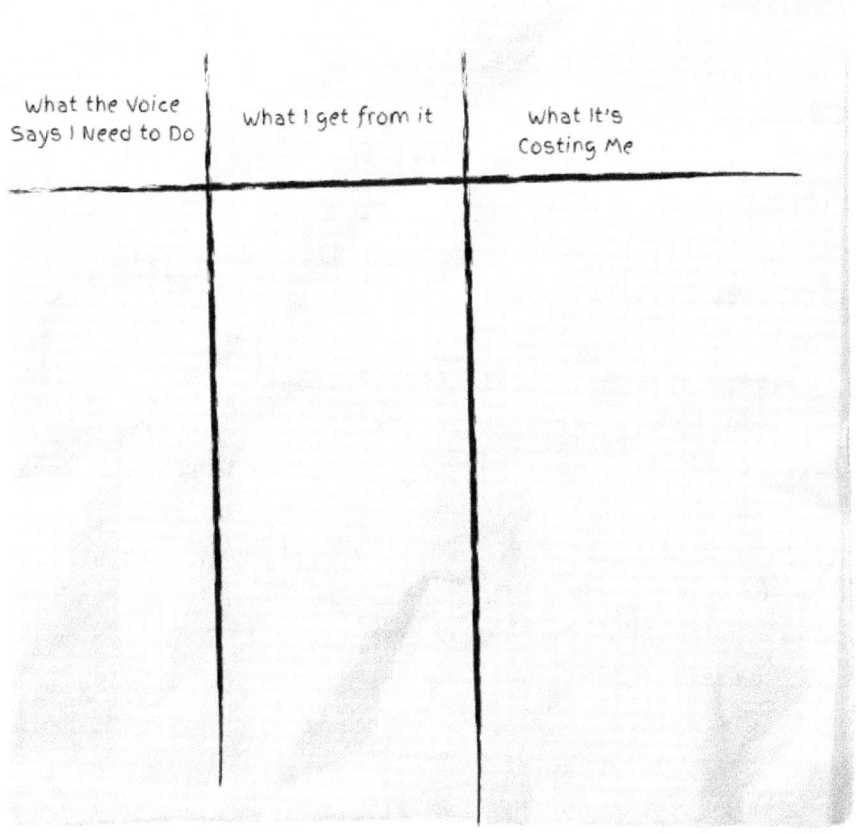

What the Voice Says I Need to Do	What I get from it	What It's Costing Me

He slid the pen across the table. "Just write the first things that come to mind. Don't overthink it."

Daniel hesitated, the Critic immediately hissing: *"This is childish. Charts on napkins? You should be sending emails, not scribbling your insecurities like a teenager."*

But for some reason, Daniel picked up the pen. He wrote in the first column:

Work more hours.

Close bigger deals.

Highlight my own wins.

Keep climbing, no matter what.

Always be beating everyone else.

In the second column, his pen moved quickly:

A big house

Vacations

Cars

Recognition

Retirement savings

"Let's pause there." John interrupted. "Before you move to the final column. Ask yourself this question. How do you know when you have crossed the finish line on those wins?"

"What do you mean?" Daniel asked.

"How do you know when the house is big enough, the vacation grand enough, cars fast enough, you know, that you have won?" John seemed genuinely curious, not trying to impose his own view on Daniel.

Daniel paused. He hadn't ever considered that before. He didn't really know. He knows that Mark's life looks really good in comparison to his own, and his neighbors and co-workers seem to have things worth chasing after. And not to mention how he saw his dad always chasing after more success. There are a lot of people who influenced his view, but he hadn't put a lot of thought into it himself.

John knew he wasn't going to get a good answer from Daniel, so he jumped back in. "I know for me, I defined wins in comparison to other people. And when I took that approach, the finish line was always moving. So that is where question three comes in. What are the costs of chasing after a moving finish line? Now, write out what you are losing."

In the third column, Daniel's pen slowed, then pressed harder as he wrote:

Missed dinners.

Disconnected from kids.

A strained and distant marriage.

Frustration with co-workers.

Constant exhaustion.

Never feeling like it's enough.

He stared at the napkin. He was rarely emotional, but he felt the need to push back tears. He hadn't expected it to look this stark when written out.

John watched quietly, not pushing or filling the silence. Finally, he said, "That's a tough scorecard, Daniel. And here's the thing: Even if you check every box in the first two columns, the third column doesn't disappear. It only grows."

Daniel looked up. For the first time, he didn't have a rebuttal, and he didn't care.

Daniel kept staring at the napkin, his lifetime of always running faster, harder, and longer boiled down to a not-so-satisfying list of accomplishments with moving finish lines. And he couldn't escape the reality of what winning was costing him.

John took a sip of his coffee, then leaned in just enough to lower his voice but still be heard. "You know what I see when I look at this?" He tapped the third column with his finger. "These aren't just costs. They're people."

Daniel swallowed hard. His co-workers, his team, Kara. Then his wife's face flashed in his mind. The kids. Even himself. The constant tension in striving to be more is exhausting.

John didn't press. He continued to let the silence linger, steady and unhurried. Then he drew a new line, creating space for a fourth column. He wrote at the top:

Who I Want to Be

What the Voice Says I Need to Do	What I get from it	What It's Costing Me	Who I Want to Be
• Work more hours. • Close bigger deals. • Highlight my own wins. • Keep climbing, no matter what. • Always be beating everyone else.	• A big house • Vacations • Cars • Recognition • Retirement savings	• Missed dinners. • Disconnected from kids. • A strained and distant marriage. • Frustration with co-workers. • Constant exhaustion. • Never feeling like it's enough.	

He slid the pen back toward Daniel and said, "I used to have a voice that was good at telling me what to do, but it never asked me who I wanted to become. But that's where the real finish line gets determined. Not where you start or the medals you collect along the way, but who you become."

Daniel stared at the blank space under "Who I Want to Be." His hand hovered, the pen tip trembling. Writing anything felt like confessing out loud, like etching failure into ink. The Critic hissed: *"Don't you dare. This will only prove how small you really are. Real men focus on results, not feelings."*

His jaw tightened. For a long moment, he couldn't move. Then, almost against his will, the pen scratched forward:

- A dad my kids actually know and enjoy.

He froze. Heat crept up his neck. Admitting that meant facing how far he'd already drifted. Still, the pen pressed on:

- A husband who's present, not just providing.
- A leader whom others want to follow and win along with him.
- A friend whom other people like being around.
- Someone at peace with myself.

When he finally set the pen down, he felt a faint release of pressure from his chest, like fresh air seeping into a locked room.

John studied the words, then nodded. "That looks a lot like a person who lives with integrity."

Daniel frowned. "Integrity? Like honesty? Doing the right thing when no one's watching?"

John smiled. "That's part of it. But I'm talking about something deeper. Integrity means being whole and living from an intentional core. No masks, no fractured versions of you being dictated by someone else's rules. The same Daniel at work, at home, and sitting in this booth. That's the kind of man people trust, and it's the kind of man who doesn't spend his life running the race following other people's rules."

The Critic stirred, bristling in Daniel's head: *"Wholeness doesn't pay the bills. Don't let him trick you. Stick to the grind."*

But Daniel didn't just absorb the Critic's voice. He questioned it because he was growing weary of how it was always sharp, always pressing for more, and making Daniel feel like he was losing.

He sat back, staring at the napkin with its four columns. For years, his scoreboard had been dictated by one voice and a series of comparisons. Now, for the first time, he wondered if there was another way to keep score. For a moment, the hum of the coffee shop dulled, and it felt like the whole place had gone still.

But then his phone buzzed. Loud. Jarring.

He glanced down — three missed calls from his assistant, followed by a text in all caps: THE BOSS IS WORRIED CLIENT WILL WALK SINCE YOU AREN'T HERE. NEED YOU NOW.

The Critic pounced instantly, voice sharp and smug. *"See? This is what happens when you slow down and play philosopher all morning. You watch the real deals slip away. You don't have time for napkins and nonsense."*

Daniel shoved the phone back into his pocket. "I've got to run," he muttered, sliding out of the booth. He grabbed his coat, barely looking at John.

John stayed calm and quiet while watching him walk away. Daniel made it halfway to the door before John shouted, "Daniel!"

He turned, appearing hurried and impatient.

John tapped the table. "You forgot this." The napkin still sat there, folded slightly at the edge like it might blow away with the next draft of air.

Daniel froze. He almost brushed it off — it's just a napkin — but something in John's tone made him retrace his steps. He reached out and picked it up and slid it into his shirt pocket.

John nodded. "Good idea. You might need it."

The Critic sneered from somewhere inside: *"What you need is to get back to work."*

But as Daniel pushed open the door and stepped into the noise of traffic, he felt the napkin against his chest — small, flimsy, but heavier than it should've been.

12

Old Habits Die Hard

The coffee shop hum faded behind him, replaced by the rush of traffic and the sharp clip of dress shoes on pavement. He thought of how he slipped the napkin into his jacket pocket, almost embarrassed by how carefully he did it, as if it were more than a scrap of paper.

The Critic was waiting.

"You really think those doodles mean something?" The voice was smooth and edged like glass. By the time Daniel reached his car, the Critic was there too, leaning against the driver's side door, arms folded. His suit was immaculate, his grin razor thin.

"You've got bigger problems than pen marks on a napkin. Did you forget the client? The numbers look great, but who is going to take the credit if you aren't there to share them? While you're playing philosopher with your new friend, someone else is getting all the credit. If the client walks, this will cost you. All this at the cost of your reputation, your career, and your future."

Daniel unlocked the door and slid inside, but the Critic slipped in too.

"Here's the truth: The only things that count are the wins you can put on the scoreboard. The wins with real numbers — deals closed, dollars banked, people impressed. And that takes certain sacrifices to run the required pace. It isn't that hard, look at all you have to show for it, and now compare that to Mark."

John's words flickered in his mind, quiet but steady, and he whispered to himself, "What if I did try to run the race differently? I am pretty exhausted."

61

He started the car, the Critic still talking beside him, but his thoughts stayed focused on what was written on the napkin, like it was an anchor.

Daniel was slowly considering the possibility that what he was doing and the way he was living wasn't really working for him. He may have some nice wins on his scoreboard, but it was clear the costs of winning were taking a toll on him in other parts of his life.

The Client Fallout or False Alarm

The office buzzed as Daniel stepped in, still feeling the folded napkin against his chest. Megan, his assistant, handed him a folder. "They're already in the conference room. Kara's been running point until you got here."

That name hit harder than the anticipated client's frustration waiting on the other side of the door. Kara. Sharp, ambitious, and recently, if Daniel was honest, one of the more vocal critics of his leadership style. "He doesn't own mistakes. He shifts the blame. Hard to trust." Her feedback following the team's last b"ig win still burned.

Daniel entered the room. The client team sat with arms crossed. Kara stood at the head of the table, mid-sentence.

The conference room felt like a pressure cooker. Slides were on the screen, numbers were good, but the client's posture said everything: Disappointed, bordering on done.

Daniel took a seat next to Kara at the head of the table, his pulse quickening. Kara was struggling to make sense of one of the numbers; things didn't seem to be adding up, and she couldn't explain why.

He knew exactly where the mistake had come from. Kara had missed a detail, an important one, and now everyone knew the mistake was there too. His old reflex rose fast: Deflect, redirect, and protect himself.

The Critic slid in, cool and smug, a voice like a whisper in Daniel's ear.

"Easy win. Point to Kara. Protect your reputation. That's how the game works."

Daniel's eyes flicked toward her. Kara was pale, braced for impact. She'd been here before — Daniel tossing someone under the bus to save face. He could see it in her jaw, tight and waiting.

For a second, he almost gave in. The Critic pressed harder.

"You'll look weak if you don't manage the situation and point the blame. Don't be naïve. Ownership is for losers. Shift the blame and move on."

But something in Daniel pushed back. The napkin. The scribbles from John's coffee shop challenge burned in his pocket like hot coal. His answer for 'Who I Wanted to Be': A leader others want to win alongside him.

He took a slow breath. "This one's on me," Daniel said evenly. "We should have communicated it earlier. I'll make sure it's corrected before next week. I know the numbers aren't adding up, but I know they are still well above last year's pace."

The words landed with a thud of surprise. The client blinked, then nodded stiffly. Not thrilled, but the tension softened. The meeting stumbled forward.

Daniel could feel the Critic raging, suit rumpled now, shouting about how this made him look weak. But when he glanced across the table, Kara's expression stopped him cold.

She wasn't gloating. She wasn't relieved. She was... startled. Her eyes narrowed, studying him, like she was recalibrating who he was in real time.

For once, she didn't look ready for a fight. She just looked at him, curious, uncertain, but with the faintest flicker of respect.

As the meeting ended, Daniel's boss whispered, "Crisis averted." As he brushed past Daniel, but in earshot of Kara as well. Daniel didn't say anything. Neither did she. But he noticed her eyes lingered just long enough to catch his eye. And in that split second, he knew: That small act of ownership had shifted something bigger than just one client conversation.

The Hallway Conversation

As the client's footsteps faded down the hall. Daniel gathered his notes with the Critic's voice still buzzing like static in his ear.

"Disaster averted? Hardly. You just branded yourself as incompetent. Kara saw it. Everyone saw it. Ownership doesn't win. Perfection does."

He shoved the papers into his folder, jaw tight, but he kept remembering the napkin. Thin, flimsy, but somehow grounding. His thoughts pressed it like a stone against the Critic's noise.

As he stepped into the hallway, Kara was waiting, not blocking, not hovering, just there, arms folded, eyes sharp.

"Got a second?" she asked.

Daniel braced himself, expecting her criticism. Old reflex response thinking: Here comes the jab, the critique. He forced a nod. "Sure."

She lowered her voice, cutting out the background hum of the office.

"You could've hung me out to dry back there."

He met her eyes. Steady this time. "That wasn't the point."

Kara tilted her head, studying him. She'd spent months writing "poor leader" in survey comments, months cataloguing the ways Daniel covered himself and let others take the hit. She had expected the same play today. She'd been ready for it.

But he hadn't. And that unsettled her more than if he had.

"Look," she said finally, almost begrudgingly, "I don't know why you did that, but... thanks."

The Critic snapped instantly: *"Don't let this fool you. She'll forget it by tomorrow. She'll still think you're a fraud."*

Daniel ignored the Critic. He just let the silence breathe.

Kara gave a short nod — not full approval, not trust, but it seemed like a start. "That kind of thing... people notice."

Then she walked away, heels sharp against the tile.

Daniel stood in the hallway, the Critic still snarling, but quieter now. For the first time in a long time, he wasn't sure which scoreboard he was keeping track of: The old one of performance at any cost, or the new one he had folded against his chest.

13

A Game Plan for a New Way to Run

Daniel's office still hummed with the aftershocks of the client meeting. He leaned back in his chair, staring at the ceiling, the napkin heavy in his pocket. He'd half expected a meltdown from Kara, but instead she'd left him in the hallway with an interaction that almost felt like... relief. The Critic wasn't quiet, though.

"Don't fool yourself," He hissed. *"One decent moment doesn't erase months of negative feedback. She'll still resent you. The client still doubts you. This napkin isn't building your career scoreboard."*

A knock at the door cut through. Daniel straightened. "Come in."

John stepped in, as casually as ever, holding a coffee cup and a brown paper bag like he had all the time in the world. "I was nearby," he said with a half-smile. "Thought I'd see how things were going?"

Daniel sighed. "Not great. Not terrible. But... a little different."

John tilted his head. "Different how?"

Daniel rubbed the back of his neck. "I didn't dodge today. My team lead, Kara, made a mistake, and we both knew it. Normally, I'd redirect the blame, push it right towards her. But I owned it. Kara saw it. She didn't look thrilled, but she didn't look crushed either. It felt... different. Like maybe I wasn't running the same way I usually do."

A slow smile spread across John's face. "You didn't treat Kara like a competitor. You treated her like a teammate. That's a shift. Same race, run it differently."

Daniel frowned. "Run it differently... but how?"

"It isn't just about the scoreboard," John said. "It's about using a different playbook. The scoreboard isn't intended to be just about more wins and medals. Your scoreboard is also measured in how you run, and who you run with."

Daniel's hand drifted to his pocket. The napkin was still there. He hadn't realized how often he reached for it now, almost like a talisman.

John noticed. "You've still got the napkin?"

Daniel nodded and slid it out, unfolding the creased napkin on the desk. The content was still clear: What the Voice Says I Need to Do. What I Win. What It's Costing Me. Who I Want to Be.

"I know you are busy, Daniel, but can I show you the playbook for running differently?"

Daniel felt a strange ease as he agreed.

John continued. "Great, before I show you the playbook for running differently, I want to give you this. If you are going to commit to the plan, you need more space than a napkin can provide."

John reached into the brown paper bag and pulled out a spiral-bound notebook with simple writing across the front cover: The GENUINE Advantage. "Now, do you have any tape in that desk of yours?"

Daniel reached inside a drawer, pulled out the tape dispenser, and handed it to John.

John grabbed the napkin from the desktop and, pulling stripes of tape from the dispenser, taped it to the first page of the notebook.

...nat the Voice Says I Need to Do	What I get from it	What It's Costing Me	Who I Want to Be
• Work more hours. • Close bigger deals. • Highlight my own wins. • Keep climbing, no matter what. • Always be beating everyone else.	• A big house • Vacations • Cars • Recognition • Retirement savings	• Missed dinners. • Disconnected from kids. • A strained and distant marriage. • Frustration with co-workers. • Constant exhaustion. • Never feeling like it's enough.	•A husband who's present, not just providing. A leader whom others want to follow and win along with him. A friend whom other people like being around. Someone at peace with myself.

"There you have it," John said. "Your first lesson in learning to run differently is now forever memorialized in your very own GENUINE Advantage notebook. Let's continue with something new."

John flipped to the next page in the notebook and began writing.

Across the top, he wrote: **RESULTS**

Down the left side, he wrote: **RELATIONSHIPS**

Then he drew a quick 2×2 matrix by drawing a horizontal line and then a vertical line that intersected it right in the middle. He then labeled the quadrants:

- **High Results / Poor Relationships** (upper left)→ *Short-lived wins* (burnout, turnover)
- **Low Results / Poor Relationships** (lower left) → *Losing alone*
- **Low Results / Healthy Relationships** (lower right) → *Warm but stuck* (good vibes, limited progress)
- **High Results / Healthy Relationships** (upper right)→ *A legacy of wins*

(trust, speed, resilience, exponential growth)

Under the box, he added three short lines:

- We don't trade relationships for results; we get results *through* relationships.
- Compete with who you were yesterday, not with everyone else. Run *with* the people beside you.
- Path to wins that outlive your life and feel GOOD → pass the batons.

John tapped the top-right quadrant. "That's where we're headed."

The Critic muttered in the back of Daniel's mind: *"Nice diagram. See if it pays the bills."*

John flipped to the next page, wrote down the page lengthwise, one letter at a time, leaving space between the letters:

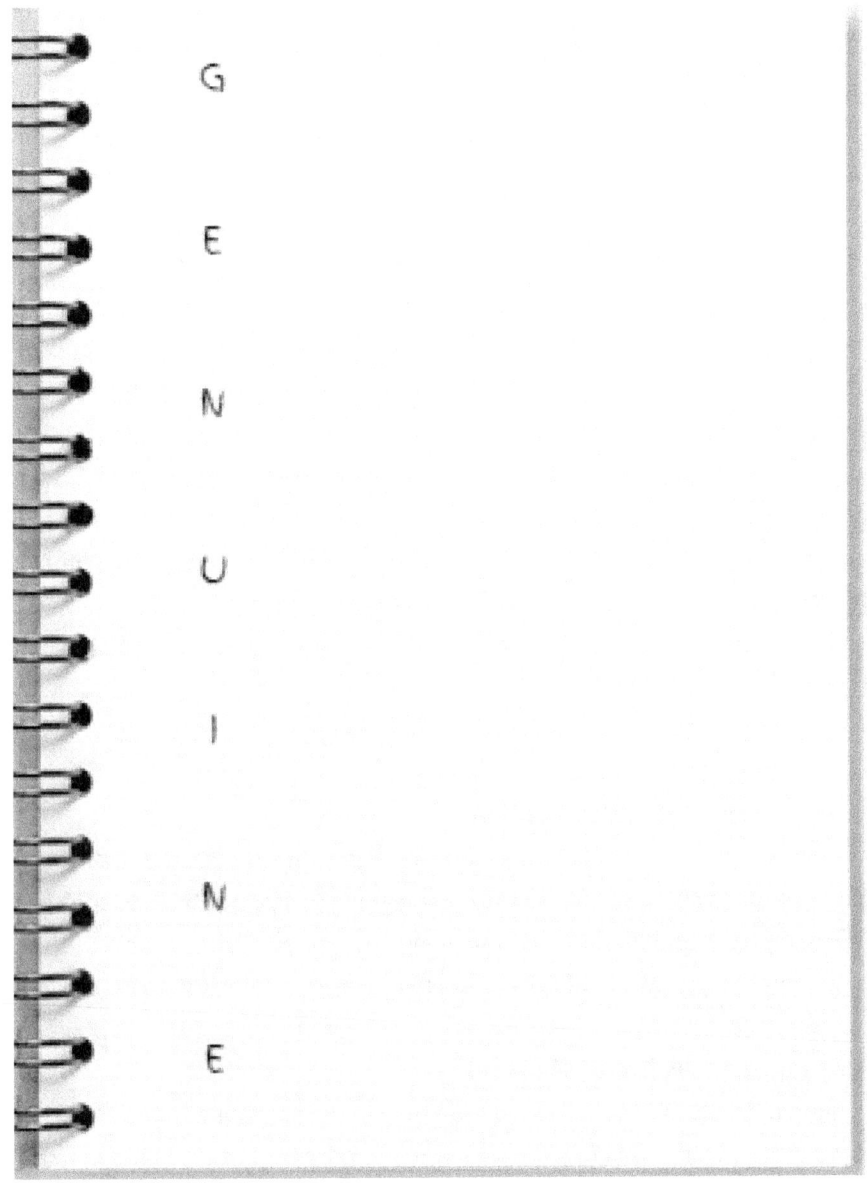

G

E

N

U

I

N

E

Daniel frowned. "That's the part of the discussion at the game I couldn't remember."

John tapped the top of the page. "GENUINE. This acronym outlines how to run the race differently. It's not based on theories or quick fixes. It's built on years of experience, tons of research, and lessons I have learned along the way. It includes seven batons you carry, pass to others, and receive from others, too. These are the principles to use if you want to win in a way that lasts. They're how you run in a way that leads to High Results and Healthy Relationships."

"And before you roll your eyes, this isn't soft. It's relational. And if you think relationships are fluff, the longest-running research on happiness and health is Harvard's study, and it says otherwise. The through line for a long, happy, and healthy life isn't income or titles. It's the quality of your relationships. People with stronger, healthier ties are happier, more resilient, and they tend to do better over time. They win and feel like winners. So, if life is a race, the factor that predicts whether you reach the finish line well isn't how hard you sprint alone, it's who you run with and how you run together. It's realizing life isn't a solo sprint but a team relay."

Daniel glanced at the letters again. "Okay. So, can you remind me what they are?"

John tapped his pen beside each letter, speaking as he wrote down what he said.

"Generous — the baton of help.

You pass credit, time, and attention so others can run. What you did with Kara, owning some of the blame, was a generous handoff. You told her, 'We're on the same team.' And sometimes you need to be willing to accept help from others. You will grow a deeper desire to do this when you focus on gratitude.

Engaged — the baton of presence.

Phones down, eyes up. Ask one more question than you answer. Presence says, 'You matter in this race.' It says you are more important to me than the next email, the next video on my social media feed, or the next thing on my to-do list. It recognizes you can't actually be mentally in two places at once.

Nice — the baton of personalized kindness.

This isn't generic politeness. It's specific kindness that names real effort. The note, the quick call, the 'I saw what you did there.' It's knowing that a person prefers tea over coffee and being recognized with kind words instead of a chocolate bar. That baton keeps people moving when their legs get heavy.

Unafraid — the baton of courage and vulnerability.

Say the hard thing cleanly; admit the miss quickly. If you only carry courage, you bulldoze. If you only carry vulnerability, you stall. Carried together, you invite people to run with you and help each other run a more sustainable race, no matter how difficult it gets.

Integrity — the baton of wholeness.

One consistent person. The same Daniel is behind the desk and at the dinner table. The same you everywhere. Show up the same no matter where you are, who you're with, or what you're doing. When your stride matches in every situation, people trust your pace.

Non-Judgmental — the baton of curiosity.

You don't know the track someone else has been on or the hurdles they have had to overcome so far. Curiosity can turn resistance into a desire to run together. Ask three honest questions before deciding whether someone is worth being on the team.

Empathy — the baton of understanding.

Try to understand people's emotions long enough to see through their eyes. Empathy isn't agreement; it's refusing to let anyone run alone, especially during times when they need the team the most. Feel first, then if necessary and equipped, fix."

He set the pen down. "That's the playbook. Not a new race, it's a new way to run the same one. And don't resist because you think these sound like principles that will only achieve mediocrity, or that other people who don't run this way will win more. There are plenty of wins to go around. You're not competing with everyone you meet; you're competing with who you were yesterday. You can help others win and let them help you, without losing a thing."

Daniel looked at the notebook, then back at John. "So, what I did with Kara...?"

"Your first baton passes," John said. "Generous and Unafraid, with a streak of Nice. You didn't protect your image (Unafraid), you protected the relationship (Nice), and you selflessly took the blame (Generosity). Over time, Kara will be willing to move faster because she knows if she slips, you will be there to pick her up. That's how teams get more efficient."

The Critic stirred, faint but familiar: *"Nice speech. Wonder if Mark is busy learning how to stop sprinting right now, too."*

John continued, "Here's how you'll know it's working," he added, tapping the GENUINE list. "Your scoreboard starts to change.

- Trust is built, so people start running at the leader's pace.
- People grow under your leadership, so an exponential amount of work gets done.
- Hard truths are spoken, enabling people to travel harder roads than they thought possible.
- Credit is shared so everyone feels like a winner.
- Repairs are made so no one feels like a failure, just a work in progress with a bright future.

Results will always matter, but when you start approaching wins like an abundant resource you achieve with people, not a scarce prize you grab from them. You find winning feels amazing. Just like you hoped it would. And when you see people as teammates instead of competitors, your finish line tends to stay consistent instead of always changing.

Daniel didn't realize he was holding his breath until he let out a deep sigh.

John laughed and kept going, "It is a lot to take in, and likely no one has ever shared this with you. Maybe you've been exposed to one point here or there at a leadership training or on a poster, but not as a packaged strategy to help you run well. I had to figure it out on my own through years of research, practicing, and making adjustments."

John paused and added one more thing. "These aren't just for work; these are for your life. You need to apply them everywhere. Today, you unintentionally put them into practice with Kara in the client meeting, but don't leave these at the office. Tonight, be intentional and try to run the race a little differently at home. Your life is a unified race. Run it consistently."

Daniel looked a little confused, so John shared an idea. "Take out your phone. You always seem to have it with you, so instead of worrying about trying to remember if you don't have your notebook with you, take a picture of the page we just laid out with the GENUINE acronym listed. You can reference it whenever you need and take pictures of the other pages as they get completed; you never know when having quick access might come in handy."

That Night — The Exchange Zone

The house was already in evening mode when Daniel walked in: A backpack by the door, a pair of small shoes tipped on their sides, and the hum of the dishwasher filling a quiet kitchen. Rachel stood at the counter, flipping through the mail. She glanced up, then back down. Not icy. Just worn.

The Critic stepped up beside him: *"She isn't in the mood for your new mantra. Don't start anything. Eat, emails, bed. Back on track tomorrow."*

Daniel slid his phone into the drawer by the stove and closed it with a soft click.

Rachel noticed. "Everything okay?"

"Yeah," he said. "I, uh... want to try something." He nodded toward the table. "Can we sit for twenty minutes? No phones. Just us."

She studied him, waiting for an explanation. When none came, she set the envelopes down. "Okay."

They sat. For a moment, the only sounds were the dishwasher and the kids laughing in the other room. Daniel felt the urge to fill the space, to brief the day, to defend his years of not-so-great behavior. He took a breath instead.

"What made you smile today?" he asked. "Not logistics. Just... something that made you smile."

Rachel blinked, surprised. Then her shoulders relaxed. "Ethan made a fortress out of shipping boxes. He called it 'The Stay-Out Dad Cave.' He only let me in because I brought crackers." A small smile tugged at the corner of her mouth.

Daniel laughed and said, "I'll be sure to bribe the guards to enter his cave."

He turned towards Ethan, who had wandered in and was now leaning on the chair, listening. "General," Daniel said in a serious whisper, "what's the fortress protocol?"

Ethan grinned. "Password changes all the time."

"What's the current one?"

"Can't tell you." He leaned closer. "But if you build a tower with me, I might make you a deputy."

"Deal," Daniel said.

The Critic cleared his throat: *"Cute. Are we done? Inbox is calling."*

Daniel ignored him. "I need to say something," he added, turning to Rachel. "Today I took the credit for a mistake at work with Kara. I should've owned more here a long time ago. I'm going to start trying to be different."

She held his eyes for a minute, searching his face the way you look at a photo to see if it's been edited. "Okay," she said apprehensively.

Ethan tugged Daniel's sleeve. "Deputy?"

"Deputy," Daniel said, standing. "But first," he looked at Rachel, "can I earn five more minutes? One more question."

"Go," she said.

"What do you need from me tomorrow night, so it doesn't feel like tonight did for you?"

Rachel thought, feeling surprised again. "If you're going to be late, tell me by four. And keep asking me one thing that I'm excited about this week. Not just how the schedule works, I liked that tonight."

Daniel nodded. "By four. And the exciting thing." He tapped the table gently, where a sprinkle of cracker crumbs mapped a little rectangle. "This is our exchange zone. I don't want to miss the handoff."

Rachel smiled small and real but firm. "Then don't."

Later, Daniel lay on the living room floor with Ethan, building a lopsided tower that leaned yet somehow kept rising. He recalled the conversation with John and the concept of a new scorecard.

He thought to himself, "Pass the batons. Be consistent at work and at home."

The tower wobbled and held. In the kitchen, the phone remained in the drawer.

14

#1: Integrity- The Baton of Wholeness

Morning light spilled across Daniel's desk with no sign of the Critic's shadow to be seen. The notebook sat where he had left it, on the corner of his desk, but it was now slightly covered by papers and folders from the week. He was looking forward to John stopping by the office for a visit.

John stepped in, closed the door, and nodded at the notebook. "How'd the handoffs go?"

"I made two," Daniel said. "I told you about Kara staying clean of the mess with the client. And that night... I put my phone in the drawer. I have been more consistent with that at home." He paused. "It felt strange, good, and new, but I survived it."

John smiled. "You didn't try to outrun anyone. You ran with them at the pace they needed." He pulled the chair closer. "Let's go deeper on one of the batons now— and we will start where everything else stands or falls."

He opened up the notebook and tapped the letter I and read: "Integrity — the baton of wholeness. One consistent person. The same Daniel is behind the desk and at the dinner table. The same you everywhere. Show up the same no matter where you are, who you are with, or what you are doing. When your stride matches in every situation, people trust your pace."

John explained, "Integrity isn't a spotless reputation or doing the right thing when someone's watching," John said. "It's wholeness showing up the same no matter where you are, who you're with, or what you're doing. At work, at home, with friends or strangers. No masks. No double lives. This requires you to let your values drive your behaviors."

Daniel frowned. "So, it's not just honesty."

"Honesty is part of it," John said, "but integrity is bigger. When you live in pieces, a portion of your energy goes to remembering which mask you're wearing. Live whole, and that energy goes back to you, becoming the best you."

Daniel stared at the notebook. The Critic tried: *"Clients don't want wholeness—they want wins. You know that sometimes it takes turning a blind eye or squinting a little, a little manipulating of the numbers, but that doesn't mean you have to do that at home too ..."*

John kept his voice steady. "Here's the trap: The world says compartmentalize. Play the game. Do what it takes to win or be liked in the environment. But that path always runs out. If people can't be sure what to expect from you, all you teach them is that they can't trust you. When people think they can't trust you, they'll stop trying to win with you."

Daniel nodded, jaw tight. "Okay. That sounds like I have a lot to change."

John replied, "It's a lot, but the challenge is worth it. Let me tell you how I started and almost stopped right away."

John's Scar: Why It Was Hard for Him

John's eyes grew distant. His voice slowed and was softer now. "You know why this one, integrity, was the hardest for me? Because I thought I could live in pieces. One version of me at work, another at church, another at home. And for a while, it looked like it was working. At the office, I was the relentless driver. At church, the dependable servant. At home, the so-called provider. Big wins at work. Big responsibilities at church. Big house at home. But none of it lined up."

He leaned back, staring at the floor as if replaying it. "I'll never forget one night. My daughter had a recital — second grade, nothing fancy, just a little school stage with a wobbly curtain. I promised I'd be there. But that afternoon, a client deal hit turbulence. I told myself, "If I just stay one more hour, I can save it." One hour became three. By the time I pulled into the school parking lot, parents were already filing out.

I walked in just in time to see Mary packing up her purse, our daughter holding her hand, still in her sparkly costume. She looked around for me, and when our eyes met... I saw the disappointment. Not anger. Not a tantrum. Just quiet, practiced disappointment."

John's jaw tightened. "At dinner later, Mary barely spoke. Finally, she said, 'I don't know who you are at work, but the man who walks through this door isn't the one I married.' Then she went back to cutting food for our son, like the conversation was already over."

The silence in Daniel's office deepened. He could picture it too clearly: The recital, the silence, the words you couldn't argue with.

"That's when it hit me," John said quietly. "I wasn't a man of integrity. I was a man of fragments. At work, I was certain to make sure I was always showing up, but at home, I was okay with being absent for things. At church, I wouldn't think of talking poorly about anyone, but in the office, it was commonplace for me to talk poorly about the so-called 'idiots'. And fragments can't be trusted. It took years to rebuild what I'd broken that night, not because of one recital, but because Mary stopped believing my promises. That's why I tell you that integrity isn't just honesty. It's wholeness. And without it, everything else eventually collapses."

The Common Objection

John leaned forward, eyes steady. "And here's what you might learn from watching how others run. The world tells us integrity is optional. People say, 'Just play the game. Do what you need to win. Compartmentalize.' They tell you results are what matter. I believed it. A lot of leaders do. But that path always runs out. Because if people can't be confident in what version of you they will experience, they learn not to trust you. And eventually, when they don't trust you, they'll stop trusting anything you build or any vision you cast."

Daniel swallowed hard. The Critic hissed again: *"Clients don't want wholeness — they want wins, he got that right."*

But John's presence, calm and unwavering, steadied the storm brewing in Daniel's mind.

The Reframing

"You think integrity costs you," John continued. "But here's the truth: It compounds. People may not always agree with you, but they'll know where you stand. Over time, that kind of consistency builds the one thing you can't buy, and that is trust."

The word lingered like a stone dropped in water, sending ripples through Daniel's mind. Trust. He realized how little of it he'd earned from Kara, from his own family. He knew he had grown into someone who played the part he thought he needed to play to get the results he wanted, no matter what.

Anchors of Integrity

John continued, "Start small, Daniel. You don't need to fix everything overnight. Integrity grows with practice. There are four anchors to build it."

Anchor #1: Establish Core Values

John leaned forward, voice steady.

"Anchor #1 is to establish your core values. Not one set for work and another for home. One set. One life. As I said, I used to live in fragments: A driven version of me at the office, a dutiful version at church, a distracted version at home. Each role had its own script. And, for a while, it looked like it was working. But it wasn't integrity. It was a performance."

He paused, his tone heavier. "The night Mary told me, 'I don't know who you are anymore' — that's when it hit me. If your kids don't recognize the man they see at work, and your coworkers wouldn't recognize the man your family sees, then you're not a man of integrity. You're an actor wearing different masks and playing competing roles."

John tapped the notebook. "So, brainstorm what values mean most to you. Not fifty values, but three, maybe four. Values that don't shift with the environment. If you choose respect, then it governs how you treat Kara in a client meeting and how you respond to Ethan when he interrupts you at home. If you choose presence, then it rules your posture in a 1:1 meeting, and when Rachel sits down to dinner at the table. Integrity is one set of values, carried into every room."

He leaned in, eyes sharp. "If you don't choose them, the world will. And the world always prioritizes busyness, image, and success at all costs. Those aren't values, Daniel. They're lies dressed up as ambition."

"So, write down Anchor #1: Establish core values. Integrity is identifying values that you will align your life around. These values are applicable in every environment."

How to Choose Your Values

John flipped to a new page and slid the notebook back toward Daniel. "Let's make this real. Five minutes."

He gave Daniel the pen. "Step one: Brainstorm and write down ten words that describe people you actually trust. Not celebrities. People you know."

Daniel started writing. Respect. Presence. Courage. Patience. Truthful... Smart

"Good," John said. "Step two: Cross out outcomes and skills. 'Success,' 'efficient,' 'smart'—those are results or talents, not values. Keep words that describe how you want to show up."

Daniel scratched a few out.

"Step three," John continued, "Circle five behavior-words that feel true and costly—the ones you'd still choose when it's inconvenient."

Daniel circled four, hesitated, and circled a fifth. Then John continued,

"Step four: Run the three tests. If a word fails any test, it's not a core value yet.

- Every-Room Test: Does this value apply in the boardroom and at your kitchen table?

- Exchange-Zone Test: Does this value clarify how you handle a handoff in a difficult situation?
- Cost Test: If this value starts to cost you important things like your speed, image, or comfort, would it still be worth it?"

Daniel nodded slowly.

"Step five," John said, tapping the notebook, "Pick three. Then write one visible behavior for each value in both rooms—work and home." If you can't name a behavior, it's not a value; it's a wish."

"There are also some pitfalls to avoid," he added with a half-smile, "Too many words, words that are really outcomes, or copy-pasting someone else's list won't work. Pick three you'll actually bring to every room. Write them like actions, not slogans."

So, Daniel wrote the following:

Respect → Work: "Don't interrupt in meetings; Ask one clarifying question."

Home: "Don't answer my phone at dinner."

Presence → Work: Establish 1:1s weekly with the team, set a shared agenda, and protect that time and the agenda. Don't just meet when things are going well (to celebrate) or just when things are going poorly (to correct). Keep them so people know they matter.

Home: "First twenty minutes after I get home, my family sets the agenda, and I follow it."

Courage → Work: "Name and address one hard truth each week, cleanly and early."

Home: "Own my tone and apologize the same day."

John leaned back after looking at Daniel's list. "That's how values stop being wall art and start being integrity. One set. One life."

Then John added, "Now here is a Micro-action to do: Tell one person at work and one person at home what your three values are, along with one behavior you're practicing today. (Example: Respect — I'll avoid interrupting in meetings and also at the dinner table.)"

Anchor #2. Align Daily Choices with Values

John's tone sharpened. "Here's anchor #2: Align your choices with those values. This one was my biggest failure. I said family was first, but when the phone buzzed at the dinner table, I always answered. Every. Single. Time. My kids learned the truth: Dad's real love is work."

He let out a long breath. "At the office, I said I cared about my team. But if a client was in the room, I steamrolled my staff to look good."

Daniel winced. He thought of Ethan tugging on his sleeve with the toy truck. He'd told himself it was bad timing. But maybe it was misaligned values.

After a silent pause, John continued, "Write this down next."

So, Daniel wrote while John shared:

"Anchor #2: Align daily choices with values. Integrity is consistency between what you say and what you do.

- Work Example: If you claim collaboration matters, don't hoard credit in front of the client. Give Kara the recognition she earned.
- Home Example: If you say, 'family comes first,' then prove it by waking up early on the weekend, not to work, but to spend time with the family. Every choice tells a story, Daniel. What story are your choices telling the people closest to you?"

John continued, "Here's a Micro-action for you to do: Identify one moment today when your actions could easily contradict your stated value (e.g., phone buzzing at dinner, client overshadowing teammate). In that moment, deliberately act in alignment with your values instead. Then jot a one-sentence reflection: Today I chose ___ over ___."

Anchor #3. Audit Your Calendar

John tapped the notebook and said, "Here's the third anchor: Audit your calendar." Daniel frowned. "My calendar? That's just logistics."

John shook his head. "No. Your calendar is a moral document. It shows your real values. Years ago, I told Mary that family was first. But one night she flipped through my planner, every page jammed with meetings, flights, and client dinners. You know what wasn't there? Not a single thing with her name on it. Not one."

He clenched his jaw. "She didn't yell. She just handed it back and said, 'I guess I know where I rank.' That cut deeper than any client critique."

John smiled sadly. "That night, I grabbed a highlighter. Green for work, blue for family, yellow for me. The pages glowed green. Almost no blue. I didn't need a lecture. The colors told the truth."

John continued, "So, add Anchor #3: Audit your calendar. If your calendar doesn't reflect your values, your life won't either.

- Work Example: Block and keep time for one-on-one check-ins, not just client calls. If people aren't on your calendar, they're not really your priority.
- Home Example: Schedule family nights, date nights, and even bedtime reading. If you leave them to when you have time, you never will."

Daniel thought of his own digital calendar and how it would be full of endless green blocks of meetings. No blue. No space. His throat tightened.

Then John added, "And here's your micro-action for today: Open your calendar and add one block (30–60 minutes) that directly reflects a core value — a 1:1 with a team member if growth is a value, a family walk if presence is a value. Don't just think about it, actually put it in writing on your calendar."

Anchor #4. Invite Accountability

John leaned forward. "And lastly, let's add anchor 4: Invite accountability. Integrity doesn't grow in isolation. It's too easy to justify ourselves. Too easy to drift."

He smiled faintly. "I gave a friend from my men's group that role. Once, after I bragged about being at all my daughter's games, he asked, 'When was the last time you stayed home, and no one had to remind you it mattered?' He saw right through me. That stung, but it saved me."

He locked eyes with Daniel. "At work, I had no one to do that. No peer who could say, 'You're chasing numbers but losing people.' So, I kept drifting until I crashed."

Daniel swallowed hard. He thought of Rachel. She no longer fought him about his late nights. She just carried the weight. Maybe she had stopped holding him accountable because she didn't think he'd listen.

John went on, "So, put down anchor #4: Invite accountability. Choose someone close enough to see your drift and bold enough to call it out (Accountability Partner).

- Work Example: Give a trusted teammate permission to ask, 'Did that decision align with your values or just your ambition?'
- Home Example: Tell Rachel and your kids they have the right to call you out if work starts winning every time. And then actually do something about it."

"Daniel," John said quietly, "integrity grows best when someone else is close enough to notice the fracture and brave enough to help you repair it. Not because they sit in judgment of what you are doing, but because they care about you and want to help you become the best version of yourself."

"Now, try this micro-action today: Send a short message to one trusted person (work peer or family member) giving them permission to ask you, 'Did your choices today reflect your values?' Then, when they ask, answer honestly by the end of the day."

Reflection

Daniel looked at the notebook carefully. His eyes were steady now.

"I want to learn," he said. "Not halfway. I mean, really learn how to run the race in the way you're talking about."

John leaned in, voice low and deliberate. "Then remember this, Daniel, integrity is the first baton. Without it, you may change how you race, but you'll always be running someone else's race. Integrity is what everything else depends on. If you can't carry this baton well, you'll drop all the others."

Daniel sat thinking about the powerful truth John shared. In this moment, he didn't feel like someone was moving the finish line on him. Instead, he felt like someone just wanted him to reach the one he was setting for himself.

John leaned back, letting the silence do its work. Finally, he added, "Is it all right if we work through the rest of the batons together over time? Each one matters. But integrity is where it begins."

Daniel nodded slowly, almost reverently. He wasn't ready to change the way he ran yet. Not fully. But he knew this was the starting line, and for the first time, maybe ever, he was ready to run at a different pace.

Daniel looked at John and admitted, "I am not sure I am fully bought in, but I am confident that what I am doing now seems to be missing something. I thought success would feel different, and at this point, I need it to feel more like I thought it would."

John spoke up, not wanting Daniel to fill any space with a change of heart, "I have been there. Let's start getting together regularly, and I will share what I have learned."

15

#2 Generosity- The Baton of Help

The next week, Daniel sat at his desk staring at the annual review forms spread out before him. He'd always hated this process: Checking boxes, writing comments, scoring people on their performance. He used to breeze through it by circling the same few phrases: "Meets expectations," "room for growth," and occasionally "exceeds." Quick, impersonal, efficient.

But today felt different. Kara's name was on top of the stack. He paused.

The Critic appeared instantly, sliding onto the edge of the desk with a smirk. *"Careful, Daniel. Don't get soft. Kara nearly cost you that client. Remember the fallout? You're still patching things up. If you're too generous here, you'll look like you've lost your edge. Be tough. Fear motivates better than praise."*

Daniel leaned back in his chair. He could still see her face from last week when he had delegated something important instead of hogging the spotlight for himself. The shock in her eyes. The way she'd nodded almost imperceptibly when accepting the assignment. It had stirred something in her and in him.

He reached for the notebook, which he was becoming more confident about having with him. He looked at G-E-N-U-I-N-E written down the side. Integrity scribbled next to the "I" then turned to the next page detailing all that he wrote down. He wondered which baton he would learn more about next.

Almost on cue, his phone buzzed with a text from John.

"Integrity starts the race. Generosity keeps you and others in it. Lunch tomorrow?"

Daniel shook his head with a wry smile. His timing was uncanny.

The next day, they sat at their usual corner table in the coffee shop. John slid his sandwich basket aside and looked at the notebook Daniel had placed on the table. He opened it and pointed to Generosity.

Daniel frowned. "Generosity? You mean like giving money? Donating to a cause?"

John chuckled. "That's one form, sure. But when it comes to running the race? Generosity is more about giving credit, giving time, giving energy, and sharing your talents. Most leaders hoard those things. They think recognition makes them look smaller, or that time spent listening slows them down, or that their skills are their competitive advantage, so they keep those to themselves. But generosity does the opposite; it increases the speed the whole team can move, it builds momentum, and it creates opportunities for others to shine so that you can perform all your leadership responsibilities."

John turned to a new page and said, "Let's dive deeper. Write the following:

Generosity, the baton of help. – Offer and accept gifts with no expectation of return. Freely giving of your time, talent, attention, and credit, and openly accepting the same help from others. You will grow a deeper desire to do this when you focus on gratitude."

He added, "Generosity isn't just about giving things away. It's also about loosening your grip so someone else can step in or you can step back."

Daniel's mind flashed back to the forms still waiting on his desk. He thought about the easy out: Circling safe boxes and moving on. But what if he actually told Kara where she had contributed, instead of only discussing where she'd fallen short?

The Critic pounced immediately in his sharp voice, *"Don't be ridiculous. She doesn't deserve it. If you start handing out credit, people will walk all over you. You'll lose authority."*

John must have seen something flicker across Daniel's face. He tapped the baton list with his pen. "Think of it this way: Integrity keeps you consistent.

But Generosity makes you magnetic. No one wants to follow a man who only takes. But someone who gives? They'll run beside him. They'll be comfortable passing the baton back and forth because when you pass them the baton, they know you trust them to carry it, and when the time is right, you will be there when they need to pass it back."

John's Scar: Why Generosity Was Hard

John's expression sobered. "But I'll be honest, Daniel, this was one of the hardest for me because generosity felt like subtraction. Like if I gave away credit, attention, or time, there'd be less left for me."

John continued, "I remember one quarterly meeting years ago. My team had pulled off a miracle. Long nights, last-minute fixes, people carrying weight I should've noticed sooner. But when the spotlight hit, I took the mic and made it sound like I had been the architect of it all. I told myself I was protecting them from blame if it fell apart. But the truth was I wanted the applause and to avoid others overshadowing my contributions."

Then John said, "A week later, one of my best managers asked to transfer. When I pressed her, she said, 'John, it feels like there's no room to grow under you. You take up all the oxygen.' That cut deep. I didn't just lose her talent when she left; I lost the trust of the team that stayed. I hoarded what should have been shared, and the room got emptier. But generosity isn't just a work thing. I was also falling short at home."

John sighed, then said, "Mary once told me, 'You're generous with money, but stingy with words.' I thought providing was enough. But what she needed was recognition. She needed to know I saw her, valued her, and noticed the little things she carried. My silence cost us more than any financial shortfall ever could."

He leaned closer. "That's the trap. We believe generosity weakens us. But stinginess shrinks you. Generosity expands you. When you give away credit, attention, or gratitude, you don't become less; instead, you exponentially grow the impact of the people around you. Generosity is what keeps people running beside you when you're out of breath because they know you are there to help them get to the next baton pass."

The Anchors of Generosity

John took a deep breath, then said with a serious tone, "I thought generosity was something I'd 'get to later,' after I'd secured success. But what I learned is this: If you're not generous on the way up, you won't suddenly become generous when you arrive. It's either built into your rhythm now, or it's missing forever. Here's what I had to relearn the hard way.

Anchor #1: Give Credit Publicly

John's voice sharpened. "Most leaders treat recognition like a scarce currency. That was me. I thought if I shared too much, I'd look smaller. For instance, if I praised someone from my team, the executives would forget that I was the one steering the ship. So, I hoarded credit. But one day, I started giving credit away. Instead of standing in front of the room and saying, 'We won.' I named names. I told the executives exactly who was contributing and how."

Then John's voice lightened, "And you know what happened? People didn't respect me less. They respected me more. The room leaned in. Eyes lit up. Because leaders who shine the light outward don't lose authority, they multiply it. People follow the ones who help them feel seen."

John's gaze grew distant. "At home, it was the same. For years, Mary carried a thousand invisible tasks — groceries, laundry, school projects. And I never named them. I thought silence was neutral. But silence is subtraction. One day, she told me, 'I feel like a ghost in this house. I keep everything running, and you don't notice.' Hearing her say that was my wake-up call. Public credit wasn't just for boardrooms. It was for kitchens and living rooms too."

Daniel thought of the time he let one of his team members share the update and take the credit with the boss. That person was so excited to be the one sharing the team's success. Maybe recognition wasn't subtraction, but instead, it was multiplication.

John pointed at the pen and nodded at Daniel to continue writing things down. "Here's Anchor #1: Give credit publicly. People live with various levels of self-doubt and worry that they are doing a good job. Take that away by sharing with them and others your gratitude. Give away credit as if it will never run out.

Work — Examples:

- Send a credit-sharing note post-meeting: Name the person and the specific contribution.
- In reviews, write one concrete sentence for each direct report's unseen win.
- In exec updates, measure your We: I ratio—aim for 7:1.

Home — Examples:

- In front of the kids, name two invisible things your spouse did that day.
- Text a parent/friend, 'You shaped me when you _____.'
- Family dinner ritual: Spotlight—each person names someone else's effort.

Here's a good micro-action for you: Find 5 people who you know have been adding tremendous value that no one else notices and send that person and their boss (if work-related) an email (or text) recognizing the contributions or impact."

Anchor #2: Live With a Mindset of Gratitude & Abundance

John leaned back in his chair, hands folded, the kind of posture he took before sharing something personal. "The next anchor is critical to passing the baton of Generosity. Live like you have enough. Enough time. Enough opportunity. Enough worth. Enough to give. That you have received so much you are thankful for, that you can't imagine keeping it all for yourself."

He paused, letting the words settle.

"When I first stepped into leadership, I operated out of scarcity. I hoarded knowledge. I guarded opportunities. I refused to give up my valuable time. I treated everything under my control like oxygen; if someone else got it, I'd suffocate. My ego was always hungry, and hungry people hold tightly to everything."

Daniel winced. That sounded familiar.

"But gratitude," John continued softly, "feeds a different spirit. Gratitude reminds you that everything you have was given, so generosity becomes natural, not forced. Scarcity says, I must protect what I have. Gratitude says, 'I'm abundantly rich, so I can share.'"

He shook his head. "Do you know what fear-based leadership produces? Quiet resentment. Withdrawal. People stop bringing their best because your insecurity tells them it's not safe."

He leaned forward, voice stronger now. "One day, my mentor pulled me aside and said, 'Real leaders aren't jealous of the light others bring; they build stages for others to shine.' That sentence humbled me. Gratitude replaced insecurity with confidence because gratitude opens your eyes to how much you already have."

John looked toward the window, remembering.

"At home, I had the scarcity mindset too. I used to walk through the door already focused on what I didn't get that day: Not enough rest, not enough peace, not enough appreciation from others. I carried the longing for what I didn't get during the day straight into my living room, and it impacted the way I behaved with my family. I was so focused on my own need for being acknowledged that I was blind to the needs of my family. I just wanted everything to be my way. I justified it by saying the energy I used was in the name of providing, so it was okay. I had nothing left to give and just wanted the world to revolve around my needs for the rest of the night."

"Scarcity questions if you have enough not just today, but into the future. Gratitude answers that question with 'I already have more than I deserve.' When you see life as a gift, then generosity becomes instinctual."

He smiled. "And here's the secret: People can feel the difference. A grateful heart creates a safe room. An abundant mindset builds belief in a shared better future. And when people believe, they are helping create a better future, and the influence of the leader multiplies. Think of it like this: When people believe they will be recognized for their effort, they are more likely to go the extra mile. It builds the belief that others notice their effort and appreciate it. And when everyone is willing to go the extra mile, you get further faster."

Daniel ruminated on all John was sharing, thinking about how many times he had that scarcity mindset- and how it affected everyone around him and everything he did. This all hit hard, as he realized that maybe abundance wasn't about having more; instead, it was about appreciating what he already had and recognizing there was plenty to share with others.

John went on, "Here's Anchor #2 to write down: Live with a Mindset of Gratitude and Abundance. Gratitude expands your view of what you have, and abundance expands your belief that you have enough to give and that there is enough to go around.

Work Examples

- When someone shines, say, 'I'm grateful I get to work with talent like yours.'
- Write a list of the experiences and people you have had that helped you grow your career.
- End each workday reflecting on something you experienced that you are thankful for.

Home Examples

- Transition ritual: Before walking in the door, say one thing you're grateful for about your life outside of work.
- Daily gratitude rhythm: At dinner, go around the table with 'One thing I appreciated today.'
- When someone helps, even in small ways, pause, make eye contact, and

say, 'Thank you. I notice you.'

This is a micro-action to help you build gratitude as your standard response to life: Start a daily routine of writing down one person, one experience, and one thing you are grateful for. Then, review the list at the end of each month. Pick people from that list to thank."

Anchor #3. Create Margin So You Can Give Energy When It's Inconvenient

John's tone grew urgent.

"Third, create margin so you can give energy when it's inconvenient. Once, I was about to leave early because I was exhausted, but then a junior staffer asked me to review her pitch deck. I was tired, hungry, and ready to go. But I saw the panic in her eyes. So, I stayed. We worked through it line by line. The next day, she nailed it and later told me that was the moment she decided to stay with the company long-term. Thirty minutes of tired energy bought years of trust."

Then John added, "But after that, I pivoted too hard and tried to make time for everyone and everything; I was always even more exhausted than before. So, I had to learn that this isn't about emptying yourself until there's nothing left. Generosity with energy isn't about running yourself ragged. It's about keeping a steady routine of resting, recharging, and protecting margin so you can give even when it's inconvenient. Think of energy like a current, not a lightning strike. The current keeps flowing. A strike makes a lot of noise but quickly burns out."

John continued, "Eventually, I realized generosity doesn't mean saying yes to every request or giving everything away. It means building enough margin to say yes when it matters most. But don't misunderstand me. It isn't as much the quantity of margin as the quality. Most people aren't going to live in perfect balance where they are guaranteed to be home at the same time every day, and their schedule is consistent every week. You create margin by reserving enough energy so you can be with people during everyday moments that matter."

John explained, "Even after I was practicing running the race differently, I still had periods when I was traveling away from home more than I was physically present. I realized I could still leverage my margin even from a distance, by saving energy for a phone call or video chat. I focused on being intentional about how I showed up with the margin I was creating instead of worrying about the quantity of time I wasn't available to give in a season. This made a huge difference."

John's voice softened. "At home, Mary used to say, 'I wish you'd give us your best energy, not your leftovers.' I didn't understand until one night I came home exhausted, and I sat in front of the TV while the kids begged me to play. I was there, but I was completely drained. So, I said, 'Hey, kids, why don't you sit with me and watch the game?' That wasn't generosity, that was scraps. Real generosity means arranging your life, so your family and your team don't just get what's left of you, but the best of you."

Daniel swallowed hard. He thought of how often he let himself get so depleted that Rachel and the kids only got the ashes of his day. Maybe the issue wasn't willingness. Maybe it was about creating enough margin.

"Here's what you need to write down." John continued.

"Anchor #3: Create margin so you can give energy when it's inconvenient. Build a routine of resting, recharging, and creating margin so you can give your best energy in the moments that matter.

Work — Examples:

- Protect a 10% buffer in your week for 'people emergencies.'
- Label three in the zone moments this week (prep, presentation, debrief) and bring full energy there.
- After big pushes, schedule a recharge block for the team; don't make them live on fumes.

Home — Examples:

- Last 30 minutes before bed = tech-free, focused planning for the next day or reflection on the current day. Clear your mind before bed. (A notepad can help to capture your thoughts.)
- Choose one recurring family moment to receive your prime energy (morning send-off, bedtime, Sunday dinner).
- Plan your rest and recharge on purpose (put it on your calendar) so your people don't only get the scraps of your day.

Here's your micro-action: Name one in the zone moment (work) and one prime-energy moment (home). Put them on the calendar."

Anchor #4. Receive Generosity Humbly

John took a deep breath before he kept going.

"And lastly, receive generosity. For years, I refused help. At home, our parents would offer Mary and me help with carrying part of the load, and I'd wave them off without even asking Mary what she thought. At work, I insisted on doing everything myself. You know what that communicated? That I didn't trust anyone else, and I believed their way would never measure up."

John continued, "One night, Mary said to me, 'We aren't partners; you just need me to do the things you don't want to do. Everything else, everything you feel is important, you hoard for yourself. You don't need me. You just need someone to watch you work.' That line cut me to the bone. Because she was right. My pride robbed her of the chance to be my partner. It robbed my work team of the chance to shine and grow."

"When I finally began letting go and allowing others to do the work, like letting Mary handle the budget her way, or letting a teammate lead a presentation without my micromanaging, I learned something shocking: They often did it better, and I even learned some things. Plus, when they didn't do well, I was able to help them grow for the next time. Receiving isn't a weakness, Daniel. It's an act of trust. And when you receive, you give others the gift of knowing you believe in their abilities."

Daniel thought of his wife offering to help with the budget spreadsheet. He'd almost brushed it off. But maybe receiving wasn't just about lightening his own load. Maybe it was about honoring the abilities of others. Then they have the opportunity to use their skills and feel like valuable members of the team, not just bystanders watching you work.

"So, here's Anchor #4: Receive generosity humbly. Receiving what others offer to do for you honors them. It says, 'You bring value, and we're in this together.'

Work — Examples:

- Delegate outcomes, not tasks. Assign what you need done, not how to do it, to someone capable of achieving the goal. Then let them do the work their way. Give space for them to learn and grow, not just execute tasks on your behalf.
- When help is offered, say 'Yes, thank you.' Full stop. No apology. No justification to protect your ego. Just gratitude.
- After a handoff, send a note upward naming the person's ownership and contribution. Give credit- not just the task.

Home — Examples:

- Let your spouse do it their way; don't 'fix' the method if the outcome works.
- Ask for help before you're underwater. Let kids carry an age-appropriate weight.
- Say out loud, 'I needed that (or I needed help). Thank you.'

And try this micro-action: Accept one offer of help without hedging and send a 2-line, thank you note about your appreciation and the value they are adding."

Reflection

John turned the notebook to face him and inspected the notes Daniel had taken.

"Generosity, Daniel, isn't about how much you can give until you collapse. It's about leading with open hands because you are grateful for all you've been given and trust that there is plenty to go around. Giving credit when you can hoard it. Giving time when you'd rather rush. Giving energy even when it's costly, but only because you've created rhythms to sustain it. And giving others the dignity of receiving their help. That's how you run with generosity. And when you do, the race stops being lonely. Because others don't just follow you, you allow them to take the lead and set the pace for a while."

Kara's Review

The next morning, Daniel called Kara into his office. She walked in stiffly, arms crossed, braced for the worst.

Instead, he slid her review across the desk. "I marked your areas of improvement, yes. But I also want you to see this," he said, pointing to a paragraph he'd written at the bottom.

Kara read silently. He had noted her calm under pressure, her ability to salvage a client relationship by adapting their presentation deck, and her steady influence on the junior associates. She blinked, eyes darting up. "You... noticed that?"

Daniel nodded. "I should have said it sooner."

The Critic seethed in the corner. *"Weak. You'll regret this."* But his voice sounded fainter, drowned out by Kara's reluctant smile. For the first time in weeks, she walked out, not defeated but energized. Daniel felt it too; the room was lighter, and the atmosphere felt steadier.

Two batons in hand now. Integrity. Generosity. The race felt different already.

Generosity at Home — Reciprocating Help

That evening, Daniel dropped his bag by the door. The house buzzed — clean clothes scattered, the smell of something half-burned in the oven, his wife juggling homework and dishes.

The Critic was quick. *"Here we go. You work all day and come home to chaos. Don't expect anything from her — she can't keep up. Just bury yourself in emails. At least there, you're in control."*

But Daniel set his phone on the counter, rolled up his sleeves, and asked, "What can I do to help?"

His wife blinked. "Honestly? I can handle the kids, but I'm late sending out the birthday invitations for Sarah's party. Would you...?"

"Sure, no problem, just point me to the envelopes and stationery, but I can't promise the handwriting will be as legible as yours."

They both laughed because no truer words were spoken. Daniel would be better off sending them out via email than trying to write in cursive.

The next morning, Daniel remembered he had forgotten to submit the budget spreadsheet he had committed to as Co-Treasurer of the Parent Teacher Association.

Rachel must have noticed a change in his face. "Are you okay?"

His instinct was to deflect. But he thought about the baton of Generosity: It wasn't just about giving; it was about loosening your grip and giving away a little bit of opportunity for others to shine.

I totally forgot to submit the PTA budget I had promised, and it is due today. My morning is totally nuts..."

Before he could finish, Rachel jumped in, "Would it be okay if your 'co treasurer' did it for you? I have time this morning after drop-off, and if you show me where the receipts are, I can figure it out."

"Thank you," he nearly shouted out of relief. "You don't know how much that helps. The receipts are on my desk in the file labeled PTA receipts."

Instead of just figuring it out and adding more stress to his day, he accepted Rachel's generous offer of assistance to get it done. She seemed excited to help, and he felt lighter. Not because he'd given away something, but because he'd accepted help and they were going to win together. He recognized her not just as someone managing chaos, but as a partner willing to help him. She didn't swoop in to rescue him; she stepped in the way partners do when they trust each other and are both focused on winning together.

The Critic grumbled in the corner. *"That isn't a partnership. That is passing on your responsibility to other people. You'd better hope she doesn't make a mistake, or everyone will blame you."* But his voice was blurred now.

Daniel realized generosity wasn't just about giving at work or home. Sometimes it meant receiving help and admitting you couldn't run alone.

He was growing in his excitement about moving away from solo sprinting towards being a man who was part of a team.

16

#3 Engaged- The Baton of Presence

The Sideline Choice —

The bleachers rattled as Daniel slid onto the bench beside John. John was glad to accept Daniel's invitation to come to his son's game. John was even more excited because Daniel wasn't arriving late; in fact, he was early. No sprint from the office, no slipping in halfway through. His son was still warming up on the field.

John gave him a sideways grin. "Two batons down: Integrity, then Generosity. How are the handoffs feeling?"

Daniel smirked. "Integrity... still messy, but real. At least I'm not juggling masks all the time, making more consistent decisions most of the time, but the pressure still sometimes pushes me to blend in. And Generosity, well, Kara actually thanked me for giving her credit. That's new."

"Not new," John said, amused. "Just overdue. Ready for the third?"

Daniel nodded but realized he didn't have the notebook. So, he got out his phone to review the GENUINE photo he had taken. The letters G E N U I N E ran down the margin, with two notations scrawled beside them:

- I — Integrity = values-led consistency
- G — Generosity = freely giving time, talent, attention, and credit

John was excited that Daniel thought of looking at the picture he took on his phone.

"Next is the first E, Type this on your notes, and you can write it out later: Engaged: The Baton of Presence –

Full attention on what matters most- Giving full attention, focusing on the most important things in the moment."

"Now," John added, "type Distraction—and you will draw a line straight through it in your notebook."

Daniel used the strikethrough feature to mark the words out as John suggested.

Almost on cue, his phone buzzed. "URGENT: Client issue — need you on call ASAP."

The Critic's voice pounced. *"See? You can't afford to sit here. Step away. Take the call. If you don't, you'll lose ground."*

Daniel's pulse jumped. He dismissed the notification and tried to refocus on the words. Integrity. Generosity. Engagement.

But just then, Daniel had an idea to pass the baton to Kara, so he quickly typed out a message.

"Kara, an urgent client need just came in. I'm at my son's game, but I know you've got this. You're ready for it more than I am right now. Keep me posted."

Her reply came fast: "Focus on your kid. I've got us covered."

Daniel smiled, then pulled his notes app back out.

John, who'd quietly watched the whole thing, nodded. "That's it. Engagement doesn't mean you ignore the world. It means you put first things first and trust the right people with the rest."

Daniel slid his phone back into his pocket as his family arrived with snacks and smiles. Down on the field, his son spotted him, eyes lighting up.

"Dad! You made it!"

Daniel stood and waved, his wife squeezing his hand.

The Critic tried to protest, *"You'll regret this, you're slipping."* But the words rang hollow, drowned out by laughter, belonging, and the slap of the ball on leather.

John's Scar: Why Engagement Was Hard

While the teams were warming up, John leaned forward, elbows on his knees. "You know why this baton nearly tripped me? Because I thought busyness looked like leadership. If my phone was buzzing, my calendar packed, my mind racing—I thought I was important. But I wasn't fully engaged in any of it. I was just scattered."

He paused. "One night, Mary told me, 'You're here, but you're not with us.' That crushed me. I'd been home for dinner, but the whole time my mind was at the office. I nodded at stories but didn't hear them. I said 'uh-huh' while scrolling emails. My kids stopped even trying. I had mastered being physically there and mentally absent. That's not presence. That's pretending."

Daniel winced. The words landed too close.

The Common Objection

John went on, "The world celebrates busyness. People brag about multitasking, spinning ten plates at once. But here's the lie: Busyness doesn't equal importance, nor does multitasking prove strength. Both of these just prove that either you don't know how to prioritize, or you don't know how to trust others. Busyness doesn't equal productivity. It equals dilution. Engagement is about depth and quality, not volume."

Daniel swallowed. He heard the Critic trying to spin it: *"If you slow down, others will pass you. If you say no, they'll replace you. If you stop to be present, you are a quitter."*

John seemed to hear it. "Engagement doesn't cost you opportunity—it protects it. Because when you focus fully on the right thing, you give it a chance to grow."

"And here is the proof I was getting it right when I started to get focused: People at work started to notice my non-anxious presence. They didn't assume I wasn't as busy as they were; they were grateful that I found time to help them through their storms, despite my own workload. Then, at home, my family noticed I was present and actually started to question if I was still employed because I wasn't always fixated on my work."

The Anchors of Engagement

"Let's dive into the anchors while we have the time.

Anchor #1. Focused Presence

John folded his hands. "Start simple. When you're with someone, be with them."

He glanced at Daniel. "I remember sitting in a conference room while a teammate pitched. I thought I was being efficient—half listening, half clearing emails under the table. Afterward, she said, 'I prepared all night, and it felt like I was presenting to your inbox.' That line broke something in me. Ten fully present minutes will build more trust than an hour of distracted half-listening."

Daniel pictured Rachel sharing the good news of her day, the way she sometimes spoke with excitement, and he answered two beats late. He heard her voice from the other night: "You weren't half-here." Maybe she'd noticed the shift already.

"So, type this in your notes:

Anchor #1: Focused presence. When you're with someone, be with them— eyes up, phone down, one follow-up question.

Work Examples:

- Step away from your desk for 1:1s so your screen isn't in view.
- Jot one phrase from what they said in your notebook and circle it to come back to later.
- In presentations, keep your hands folded or on the table instead of hovering over your keyboard.

Home Examples:

- Put your phone in another room during dinner and notice the difference in your listening.
- Repeat back one part of a child's story ('So you were the goalie?') before asking your next question.
- Practice leaning in physically—knees and shoulders pointed toward the person you're talking with.

And here's your micro-action: Put your phone out of reach for your next conversation. Ask one follow-up question and repeat one phrase back."

Anchor #2 Boundaries as a Gift

"Second—boundaries," John said. "Engagement requires saying no so you can fully say yes."

He smiled without humor. "I used to treat boundaries like walls that kept people out. Now I see them as fences that keep what matters in. The turning point? My son's playoff game. An executive pinged me ten minutes before first pitch: 'Can you jump on real quick?' Old me would have stepped onto the concourse and missed the inning. That day, I texted him that I was at my son's game, and I would send a summary of the current status by 4 and join a call first thing in the morning. I expected backlash. Instead, I got, 'Thanks for the heads-up. Enjoy the game.' Turns out clearly communicated boundaries with an action plan can actually earn respect."

He glanced at Daniel. "Boundaries aren't selfish—they're generous. They give your best attention to the people and priorities that matter most."

Daniel let out a slow breath. Boundaries had always felt like weakness to him; no one else seemed to have any, so why should he go first? Maybe they were more about strength in disguise.

"So, here's anchor #2: Boundaries as a gift. Say "no" on purpose so your "yes" can be real. Boundaries protect presence.

Work Examples:

- Block 90 minutes of 'focus work' on your calendar and treat it like an external meeting.
- Write a boundary script: 'I can take this on if we shift timeline X or move Y.' Use it in your next request.
- Protect your commute—listen to a podcast or music that transitions you into/out of work mode.

Home Examples

- Create a first-hour home rule where no work emails are opened.
- Build the ritual that all dinners are phone-free zones.
- Be willing to say no to social events without the fear of missing out (FOMO), so you have room to breathe.

Try this micro-action: Write your boundary script and use it before the day ends."

Anchor #3. Mental Toughness and Speed Through Single-Tasking

"Third—train your mind," John said. "I had to learn to do one thing at a time."

He shook his head. "I wore multitasking like a badge. I'd fire off emails, mid-meeting, and tell myself I was efficient. Then I missed a simple detail that cost us a week. My mentor said, 'You're busy, not tough.' Focus is like a muscle that you need to build and strengthen. Finishing what's in front of you before moving on—that's mental toughness. It stops you from always trying to endure chaos; it means creating clarity."

Daniel pictured the constant ping of his inbox, the thrill of being fast or first, followed by the fatigue of being fractured. How many times has he had to restart something because he lost his place trying to win at the newest distraction disguised as an urgent request?

"So, add Anchor #3: Mental toughness and speed through single tasking. Focus is a muscle. Finish one thing before starting the next.

Work — Examples:

- Run a 25-minute single-task timer (Do Not Disturb mode). Summarize output in 3 bullets before switching.
- Email in two chunks (late a.m., late p.m.) instead of constant toggling.
- Reserve instant messages for conversations or questions that require an instant response. Otherwise, save yourself and others from an interruption and DON'T SEND IT.

Home — Examples:

- Do one chore start-to-finish (dishes, lunch prep) without hopping between them.
- Play a 10-minute single game with your kid, no multitasking. Your full presence will be felt more than hours of your distracted presence.
- During a talk with your spouse, don't fix—finish listening.

And here's your Micro-action for the day: Pick one task. Start a 25-minute timer. No switching. End by sending out one visible result, no matter how small it feels."

Anchor #4. Everyday Connection

"And last, don't mistake being engaged with showing up only when the scoreboard is on. I used to show up big for the high-stakes moments, presentations, deadlines, and even family milestones, but I'd miss the everyday connections. A walk, a late-night talk, a check-in text. Engagement isn't about the highlight reel. It's about the daily habits that say, 'I see you; I'm with you, and you matter.' Off-field connection is what proves engagement is real."

Daniel felt his throat tighten. He thought of Ethan tugging on his sleeve weeks ago, toy truck in hand. He'd missed it. But tonight, at the ballfield, maybe he'd started to redeem it.

"So, add Anchor #4: Everyday connection. Engage outside the highlight reel. Small and steady intentional choices will prove that the person matters.

Work — Examples:

- 3-2-1 weekly cadence: 3 check-ins (personal, not work focused), 2 gratitude notes, 1 no-agenda coffee.
- Once a week, ask someone in passing: 'How's life going?' then listen to the response.
- During work, and not just in crisis or celebration moments, check in on how things are going with your team. (Ex: What is going well, what are you worried about, what help do you need?)

Home — Examples:

- Walk-and-talk after dinner once a week, so you can talk without the distractions of home.
- Leave a note (on the fridge, in a backpack, on a pillow) that says, 'Thinking of you.'
- Start a small weekly tradition (Saturday pancakes, bedtime song, Sunday call).

And here's a good micro-action to try: Send one no-agenda check-in within the next hour. Only check in on the person, not their projects."

Play Ball

The umpire screamed, "Play ball!" And just like that, the conversation ended just in time for the game to start. Daniel was appreciative of this instant opportunity to practice being engaged by watching his son play the game he had loved as a child. Daniel vowed this would become a more intentional part of his routine; to create margin in his calendar so he could soak in moments watching his son learn to love the game, too. And at least for today, Daniel was keeping that commitment.

After the Game

When Daniel pulled his phone out to transfer his notes into the notebook, he was expecting to see a mess of urgent texts. Instead, the screen lit with a single text from Kara:

"Handled it. Client happy. Honestly, it was good for me to take the lead. Thanks for trusting me."

For a moment, he just stared, thumb hovering. Something inside him shifted. Not too long ago, he would have assumed only he could fix things. Tonight, Kara's voice carried confidence and gratitude.

The Critic whispered sharply: *"Lucky break. Next time, you'll pay for handing things off."*

But Daniel shook his head and thought to himself. "Or maybe next time, someone else will shine again. Maybe that's the point."

He set the phone down just as his wife walked into the room, still carrying the smell of popcorn from the game. She leaned on the doorframe, studying him.

"You were different tonight," she said.

"Different how?"

"Usually, even when you're sitting with us, I can tell part of you is somewhere else, checking email, running through work in your head. But tonight... You were 100% there with us." She smiled, softer now. "It felt good."

Daniel exhaled, almost laughing at the relief in it. "It felt good to me, too."

She walked toward him and kissed him on the cheek. It was a simple gesture, but it landed like a promise.

Daniel smiled while he continued transferring his notes into the notebook.

Reflection

Later, as the house settled into quiet, Daniel picked up his phone again and typed a simple message:

"Thanks for pushing me, John. Engagement hit different tonight. Ready for the next baton whenever you are."

Daniel sent the text, smiling faintly to himself. For the first time, he felt like he wasn't just surviving the race. He was learning how to run it.

A buzz came back almost immediately.

"Proud of you," John wrote. "Engagement means presence. Tonight, you gave your best to the ones who matter most. That's how you build a life that lasts. Keep going. The race isn't about speed—it's about who you're running with and getting to the finish line together."

Daniel set the phone on the nightstand, the Critic's voice nearly drowned out by Kara's gratitude, his wife's smile, and John's steady words. For now, the room was filled with peace, and so was he.

17

#4 Nice- The Baton of Personalized Kindness

The Coffee Shop

Daniel arrived at the corner coffee shop earlier than usual, with his coat collar pulled up against the light drizzle of rain. John had invited him again, and Daniel smiled to himself at the predictability of their rhythm: John usually strolled in late, cheerful and unhurried, while Daniel, still wired to corporate timelines, arrived early and ready.

But today he decided to do something different. As he stood in line, the barista smiled and asked, "The usual?"

Daniel almost said yes, then paused. He glanced at the menu, then he remembered that John always ordered the same thing: A dark roast blend with a splash of cream, no sugar. And he often added a breakfast sandwich with egg and cheese on ciabatta. Daniel had teased him once about being a creature of habit.

Now, instead of his own order, Daniel pointed at both. "I'll take the sandwich and the dark roast with cream. And… I'll grab another black coffee for me."

When John finally appeared, brushing rain off his jacket, Daniel already had the tray on their table.

John stopped in his tracks, grinning. "Well, now. Look at this." He picked up the cup of coffee and raised it as if he were giving a toast. "That, Daniel, is being nice."

Daniel chuckled. "Just thought I'd save us some time."

But John leaned forward, tapping the table for emphasis. "Don't shrug it off. That right there is more than convenience. That's personalized kindness. You didn't just grab any coffee; you remembered what I like. You thought about me. You gave me what I actually wanted, not just what was easy for you. That's what 'nice' really means: Noticing someone enough to give them what they need in a way that fits them."

Daniel sat back, taking it in. For years, he had thought of being nice as little more than manners, such as holding doors, saying please, and offering generic compliments. Useful, yes, but hardly powerful.

John seemed to read his thoughts. "Nice isn't generic politeness. It's intentional, thoughtful, and personal. That's why it matters."

Daniel nodded slowly. He pulled out the notebook and turned to the page with G E N U I N E written down the side. Three batons had already been covered: Integrity, Generosity, and Engagement. Under John's guidance, he was ready to fill in the fourth.

Daniel flipped to a new page as John began, "Okay, let's get this down. #4 Nice: The Baton of Personalized Kindness. Offer kindness in the way others need it most—specific, thoughtful, and personal."

He then said, "Underline the word personal. It's just like I mentioned to you about the coffee and the sandwich. Having you remember my order tells me you have been paying attention throughout all our meetings here. You noticed things about me, and then, when the time was appropriate, you put what you learned into action. THAT was specific, personal, and thoughtful."

John's Scar: Why Nice Felt Weak

John leaned back in the booth, eyes narrowing slightly. His voice softened. "But let me tell you something, Daniel. For a long time, I thought kindness was weakness."

Daniel raised an eyebrow. "Really?"

"Oh, yes. I figured nice guys got walked over. So, I played it safe—polite nods, surface pleasantries, the occasional handshake. Nothing more."

He took a sip of his coffee, then stared at the table as if rewinding years.

"One of the hardest moments of my career was when a team member I barely noticed resigned. I thought she was leaving for more money or a bigger opportunity. But in her exit interview, she said: 'I don't think you ever actually saw me. You said hello, but I never felt known. I think this might be the first time we have even sat down together.' That gutted me. I had worked hard, driven results, grown revenue—but I never offered her any personalized kindness. She didn't quit the job. She quit me."

Daniel winced.

"And that wasn't the only problem I encountered. I wasn't intentionally mean; I had just learned kindness didn't matter. Earlier in my career, I tried to be kind. I bought coffee for the team and remembered birthdays. But one guy mocked me, calling me "The Office Dad," so I shrank back. This made me think that leaders can't be nice because they look soft. So, I pulled away, convincing myself it was safer to wait for others to go first and match their kindness with some common impersonal courtesies."

He leaned in now, voice firmer. "But here's the truth: Withholding kindness cost me more than giving it ever could. I kept people at arm's length. I lost loyalty. And at home…" His voice faltered. "At home, it nearly cost me my marriage."

John sighed and continued, "One night, Mary looked at me across the dinner table. The kids were half-focused, homework was scattered everywhere, and she just said, 'You're respected at work, and I bet your best people know they matter, but I don't feel cherished at home.' That hit like a hammer. I had confused providing with cherishing. I was polite. I was present in my duties. But I wasn't kind in a way that felt personal. I didn't notice the flowers she had planted to make the landscape look nice. I didn't learn her signals about what would make her feel loved. That was the moment I realized personalized kindness wasn't weakness at all; it was an intentional investment in others. And I had neglected it for years, so instead of having relational capital, I was in debt."

The words hung between them, heavy but alive.

As John finished his point, Daniel's phone buzzed on the table. A group text from the office: "Need update on client deck. URGENT." His fingers twitched. The Critic pounced, *"See? This is why 'nice' doesn't matter. Direct communication does, so you know exactly what they need. Do you want to be remembered for donuts or for deals? Stop wasting time—answer them before someone else takes the credit."*

Daniel stared at the phone, then at John's coffee in his hand, half empty. The choice sharpened: Will he choose efficiency or kindness?

In this moment, he didn't have to choose, as a new message appeared; it was Kara. It just said, "I have the numbers we need."

He slid the phone face down, knowing the team had the answers, and leaned in.

The Critic hissed again, *"You'll regret this. How long before they just go right to Kara and they realize they don't need you?"* but Daniel noticed something shift inside. He had chosen presence.

The Cultural Objection

"But isn't there truth in what people say? That nice guys finish last?"

John gave a wry grin. "That's the objection, isn't it? It gets ingrained in us that being kind makes us soft. If we make kindness a priority, then people will take advantage, and we will lose our edge. And if we pick people over progress, then we lose. People see kindness as a barrier to success."

He shook his head. "But here's the reality: When people experience your care through personalized kindness in actions and words, they lean closer and dig in deeper. Kindness is like a flywheel. An isolated act of generic kindness won't have a lasting impact; it might even catch people off guard. But if you make it a consistent habit, the return on your investment is unbelievably high. True intentional kindness is a multiplier, and it really is contagious. It's the kind of thing that once it starts to spread, everyone catches it."

He leaned in. "Fear motivates for a quarter. Kindness motivates for a career. Kindness isn't fluff, it's fuel."

John continued, "I knew a manager once who was sharp and hard driving. He got results by fear. People hit deadlines because they didn't want to be yelled at. And yes, on paper, he looked good. But the moment people had another option, they left. He never built loyalty."

Then John shared, "Contrast that with a leader I met years later. She wasn't flashy, but she remembered birthdays, she checked in on people to see if they needed help, and she noticed when someone had been unusually silent in meetings. Ten years later, her old employees still called her for advice. Which leader was successful?"

Daniel thought of his first boss, who had a way of always gathering the most talented team members. It didn't seem to matter that he wasn't the most technically strong, but he really knew how to bring people together and achieve amazing things. He would often say it was more important as a leader to know your people and make them feel seen than to know everything about the work and nothing about the workers.

John added, "Sports prove the same point. A coach who only yells at the players gets their effort in the moment, but as soon as he moves on to the next player, the effects fade. But a coach who knows their players and reaches them on an individual level will get their commitment for a lifetime."

"What you need to internalize is that kindness isn't about ignoring problems or pretending everything is okay, when everyone knows it's not. That is the kind of fake niceties that cause people to believe nice guys finish last. We are talking about noticing the people who are on your team in ways that let them know they matter and you care about them. This pays dividends in the moments when you need to push people harder or share difficult messages about performance because people know you care about them, not just the results. Kindness isn't ignoring reality, it's igniting the relationships that inspire."

The Anchors of Kindness

Anchor #1. Notice, Personalize, and Speak with Specifics

John continued, "People feel valued when you notice what others ignore—and when you deliver that attention in ways that matter to them. Learn their coffee order, their kid's name, and their favorite donut. Notice what makes them different—the designer's eye, the analyst's instinct, the quiet stabilizer. It's not about the object or the trait—it's about the attention. Noticing details says: You matter enough to be remembered. Celebrating uniqueness says: I see what makes you, you."

Daniel thought back to when he'd breezed past Susan, a junior associate, not remembering she was overwhelmed by her mom's illness. He never once asked how she was doing, even though he had just signed up to donate a gift card to help her family out. Susan wanted acknowledgement and support, but instead, she felt invisible.

John kept going strong with his words, "It isn't just about noticing, you need to speak the specifics—and deliver them in the language people actually receive. General praise is cheap. Anyone can offer a simple, 'Good job.' But specific kindness is powerful. Tell someone that the way they caught that error saved your company a client. Or that the patience they showed in a situation resolved that conflict. Being specific proves you really noticed what they did."

He paused. "And here's the part most people miss: Everyone receives kindness differently. Some light up with words of affirmation, others with quality time, others with practical help or small surprises. If you only give kindness in your language, you'll miss them entirely."

Daniel thought of one of his associates, Jesse, who would always ask for feedback. He knew what made her different; she could really hold a room of people's attention, but he had never told her that directly. He figured she probably already knew it. And his wife, Rachel, certainly knows Daniel needs her, but how many times had he tried to show that by bringing small gifts home from business trips? In this moment, he realized that maybe those gifts missed the mark, and that's why she never really seemed as excited about receiving them as he was about giving them to her. He was noticing—but not giving her what she personally needed.

Daniel was also horrified to think about how many times his kids would try to share something they were proud of, and he would simply answer back with one-word responses like "nice job" or "good work," instead of commenting specifically on the details of their story.

John pointed to Daniel's pen and said, "Add this to your notebook:

Anchor #1: Notice, personalize, and speak with specifics. Notice what makes people unique, then deliver kindness in the language they receive best—with precision and personal attention.

Work — Examples:

- Keep a private 'People Notes' list: Specific coffee orders, kids' names, recent surgeries, passions, and unique strengths.
- When recognizing someone, use the formula: 'When you ____ (behavior), it ____ (impact).'
- In 1:1s, ask, 'What feels most encouraging—words, time, help, or shared moments?' Then act on it.
- In reviews, add a line: 'Your superpower this season has been ___.'

Home — Examples:

- Replace 'How was your day?' with something specific like, 'How did the field trip go today?'
- Ask, 'When do you feel most cared for—words, time, help, or little surprises?' Then give it in that form.
- Name a child's or spouse's signature strength in front of the family.
- Step into their world and join their game, hobby, or project.

And here's a good micro-action: Write one line that starts, 'I noticed ____, and it mattered because ___.' Then ask one person, 'What makes you feel most seen—words, time, help, or shared moments?' Deliver both before the day ends."

Anchor #2. Anticipate Needs: Act Before You're Asked

John smiled, swirling the last sip of his coffee. "There's one more layer to kindness most people never reach. The best kindness doesn't wait for an invitation—it arrives early."

Daniel tilted his head. "You mean, like guessing what people want?"

John shook his head. "Not guessing. Knowing. Kindness rooted in attention starts to notice patterns. You see the late-night texts before a deadline and realize someone's carrying more than they'll admit. You stock the breakroom before they run out. You ask the question before they have to explain. Anticipating needs says, 'I'm paying attention to your world, not just my own'"

He paused, then added quietly, "At home, it's the same. You know what love looks like when you walk into the kitchen and realize the sink's full, so you take care of it. Or when you bring the blanket before she shivers. These things don't take money or brilliance—they take awareness. One of the highest forms of kindness is anticipation."

Daniel thought about the difference between being responsive and being ready. He'd spent years reacting well—but John was describing something deeper: Relational foresight.

John continued, "So let's add anchor #2: Anticipate needs: Act before you're asked. Thoughtfulness is the highest form of kindness.

Work — Examples:

- Restock a shared resource before someone has to ask.
- Send prep notes or reminders before the team realizes they need them.

- Ask, 'What will make next week easier for you?' Then act on the answer.

Home — Examples:

- Set out your partner's coffee mug or prep the morning task they dread.
- Check the calendar for stressful days and lighten their load in advance.
- Do the non-urgent thing before it's mentioned.

Do this micro-action: Ask yourself, 'Who might need something tomorrow that I can do today?' Then quietly do it."

Anchor #3. Small Sacrifices and Micro Actions

John continued, "Kindness often means there will be a slight inconvenience to you, but a great relief to someone else. Hold the door. Give them the better seat. Step back so they can step forward. They are small costs with big echoes. Leadership isn't about reserving your place at the front of the line. It's about making space so others can breathe."

"The goal of kindness isn't to make up for poor behavior or gain favor for the future; it's about making others know they matter to you. This is best done through consistent actions on a regular basis."

"One thing to remember is that the goal of being nice is to build the team, not manipulate others or keep a secret scorebook. If you ever find yourself focused on being nice to win others over or keep a record for future favors, you aren't being nice, you are being manipulative."

Daniel thought about the times from his childhood when his mother would bring him a popsicle on warm days when he had been outside for hours. He never had to ask for them. He had no expectation she would bring them, and it didn't cost her much. But he felt really loved, especially since she often brought him the orange ones, which were his favorite flavor. Maybe John was right, little actions go a long way.

"Now let's dive in and write this all down," John said, as Daniel grabbed his pen again.

"Here's anchor #3: Small sacrifices and micro actions. Consistent micro actions are better than occasional grand gestures.

Work — Examples:

- Carry the laptop and let someone else lead the presentation.
- Bring the team a snack (a variety of their favorites).
- Offer to do the unglamorous task no one wants this week.

Home — Examples:

- Take the late-night clean-up so your spouse can sleep.
- Give the better seat, the last slice, the parking spot.
- Pause your scroll to go join the game outside or on the floor now, not later.

Practice this micro-action: Choose one two-minute sacrifice. Do it without announcing it."

Anchor #4: Return and Sustain: Follow Through Builds Trust

John leaned back, his expression growing more serious. "Now here's where most people lose the race. They notice things only once. They're kind in the moment. But then they move on and never circle back. Kindness without follow-through is just a pleasant interruption."

Daniel frowned. "What do you mean?"

"Take Susan, for example," John said quietly. "You donated that gift card, right? That was generous. But did you ever ask her how her mom was doing a week later? A month later?"

Daniel's face fell. He hadn't.

"That's the gap," John continued. "One-time kindness feels nice. But sustained kindness builds trust. People need to know that your attention isn't performative—that you remember what mattered to them last week, and even last month. That you return to the conversations others forget."

He paused, swirling his coffee. "At home, it's the same. How many times have your kids told you about something they were excited or nervous about—a test, a game, a friend situation—and you nodded, but never asked about it again? They're watching to see if you really cared or if you were just being polite in the moment."

Daniel thought about Ethan mentioning tryouts for the soccer team two weeks ago. Daniel had said, "Good luck, buddy." But he never asked how it went. The shame hit him like a weight.

John's voice softened. "Leadership isn't just about showing up once. It's about showing up again. The most powerful form of kindness is the kind that returns. It says, 'You weren't just a task on my list. You're someone I actually care about enough to follow up.'"

Daniel nodded slowly, the truth sinking in.

John continued, "So let's add Anchor #4: Return and sustain: Follow through builds trust. Kindness that circles back proves it was never just a gesture—it was genuine care.

Work — Examples:

- Circle back on conversations. 'Last week you mentioned the client presentation was stressful—how did it go?'
- Don't just say 'Let me know if you need help'—check in proactively next week.
- Reference history in 1:1s: 'You were worried about that deadline last month. Has the workload eased?'
- Complete what you offer. If you said you'd send a resource, send it.

Home — Examples:

- Ask about the thing they mentioned yesterday: 'Did your friend respond to your text?'
- Keep small promises: 'I said I'd look at that link—let me do that now.'

- Acknowledge milestones you discussed earlier: 'Wasn't today the exam you were nervous about?'
- Return to hard conversations instead of letting them fade.

Do this micro-action: Identify one conversation from this week that needs follow-up. Return to it today with genuine interest."

Daniel stared at his notebook. Four anchors. Four ways to make kindness more than a moment—to make it a pattern that builds real connection.

Little Gestures, Big Echo

Daniel was feeling good. He had now filled multiple pages with notes and ideas for how to run the race differently. Four batons and their accompanying anchors were inspiring him with hope to make these changes.

The next morning, Daniel carried the pink pastry box into the office. Susan smiled at her chocolate glaze. Mike reached for a jelly-filled, and Kara lit up at her cinnamon twist.

"Wow, that was so thoughtful of you to do this," Kara said.

Daniel shrugged. "Felt like the right thing."

The Critic snarled this time, louder than before: *"Cheap sugar won't make them respect you. They'll roll their eyes when you leave. Leaders don't earn loyalty with sprinkles."*

But the laughter spreading through the office drowned him out. For once, Daniel realized how empty the Critic's voice sounded against genuine joy.

Later, Daniel left a thank-you note. Held a door longer. Asked about a coworker's son. Each effort was small. But together they echoed.

Kindness with His Children

That evening, Daniel tried something new at home. Instead of one blanket gesture, he studied each child. Ethan loved roughhousing. So, Daniel dropped onto the floor and wrestled with him. His daughter loved telling stories, so later he sat with her, listening intently as she retold her day.

Different gestures. Same kindness. He realized the baton didn't look identical in every hand—it had to be passed in their language.

Rachel noticed from across the room. She smiled quietly, with her sketchbook open.

Closing Reflection

Later, Daniel texted John:

"Tried personalized kindness. Rachel's sketchbook is back on the table. Kara laughed over her donut. My kids lit up at simple moments. It feels like connections, not just gestures."

John replied:

"That's it, Daniel. Nice doesn't mean weakness. It's the strongest quiet force in the room. Fear may win compliance, but kindness wins hearts. And hearts build legacies. Personalized kindness scales from coffee shops to offices to homes to communities. Never underestimate it."

Then John added, "Remember, this baton carries people further than fear ever will. Fear is a solo sprinter's approach; nice is required for handoffs as we run the relay together. Pass it forward, and you'll see it multiply long after you've run your leg."

Daniel set the phone down, with his heart lighter. The Critic was nowhere to be found. He thought of Kara's laugh, Rachel's sketchbook, and his kids' smiles. Kindness wasn't fluff. It was fuel.

18

The Mid-Year Review

Daniel sat stiffly in the chair across from his boss, while feeling the windowless conference room pressing in on him. A neat stack of reports sat between them, but his boss didn't bother opening them.

"Daniel," his boss began, voice even but cutting, "I've got to be honest. There's a perception you're slipping. Clients notice Kara stepping in more. You're not as visible. They want you at the helm, not your protégé. And frankly, your peers are starting to wonder where your focus is. Plus, you made that mistake at the client meeting a few weeks back. We promoted you because you clearly demonstrated a strong understanding of what it takes to succeed here. Now it feels like maybe it was too soon."

The words landed like body blows: "Slipping. Not visible. Wondering where his focus was. Not a winner. Too soon."

And then—he heard it again.

That familiar sneer of the Critic curling in his mind.

"I knew it. You've been playing at this new soft version of yourself—handing things to Kara, going home earlier, listening to that old man, and learning from him. And what did it get you? Exactly what I told you. Weak. Distracted. Irrelevant."

The Critic was back. Stronger than he'd been in weeks.

Daniel gripped the arms of his chair, pulse quickening. His throat felt tight, like every defense he could give would sound hollow. For the first time since beginning to apply the GENUINE approach, he felt completely lost. He was trapped between the boss's disappointment, the Critic's scorn, and John's GENUINE way to run.

He muttered something vague, something safe: "I hear you. I'll take that feedback seriously." His boss nodded, but the disappointment lingered in the air like a thick fog.

When the meeting ended, Daniel walked out, shoulders heavy. He was anxious to get back to his desk and open the notebook. He didn't know what came next. Integrity. Generosity. Engagement. Nice. He had practiced those. But at this moment, this sting didn't fit with any of the concepts he had already learned.

At his desk, he pulled out his phone and texted John:

"Rough review. My boss thinks I am not a winner, and I have been slipping. He questioned my commitment. I really need guidance."

He stared at the screen. No dots appeared. No reply. Only silence.

A soft knock on his office door pulled him out of his spiral. Kara stepped in. Her usual confidence was there, but her eyes searched his face.

"Hey," she said carefully. "I heard you just came out of the review. How'd it go?"

Daniel's throat tightened.

This was the fork in the road. He could pretend—flash a rehearsed smile and say, "All good, just the usual feedback."

Or he could risk it. Tell the truth and admit that he was questioning whether he'd made the right call in giving her so much freedom.

The Critic's voice attacked again. *"Don't you dare say anything. Smile, nod, act like everything's under control. If she thinks you regret handing her responsibility, she'll lose respect for you. And if you tell her the truth? She'll see you as weak. Remember what your boss just said, you are slipping."*

Daniel exhaled, long and shaky. He looked at Kara—really looked. She wasn't there to undermine him. She was there because she cared, because she noticed he was different. He wondered if her caring presence was the result of the changes he's made.

"I'll be straight with you," Daniel said finally. "Boss thinks I'm slipping. That I've handed off too much. That you're doing more than me. And part of me… part of me wonders if I did the right thing giving you so much responsibility."

The words hung in the air. Raw. Risky.

Kara blinked, surprised, then pulled up a chair.

"Daniel… do you know what it's meant to me that you trusted me with more? That you didn't just hoard all the work to prove you're the guy? Clients respect me because you gave me a chance. And honestly—it's made me respect you more, not less."

Daniel swallowed hard. The Critic prepared to mutter one last protest, but its voice had already faded into the background.

Kara leaned in. "I know today stings. But you didn't make a mistake by trusting me. You made me better—and in the long run, that makes us stronger."

Daniel sat back, letting her words settle. The Critic tried to whisper again, but it was drowned out by something steadier—gratitude.

"Thank you," Daniel said quietly, then, with more strength, he continued, "Really, Kara. That means more than you know. And I need you to hear this from me—you've shown up in ways that make a real difference. Not just in the work, but in the way people depend on you now. I can't tell you how much I appreciate that we can count on you."

Kara's shoulders straightened, her eyes brightening.

Daniel continued, "And if I'm going to keep supporting you the right way, tell me—what's something I should keep doing to help you grow? What's been most helpful?"

For a moment, Kara looked down, thoughtful. Then she smiled. "Honestly? Keep trusting me. Keep giving me room to stretch, even when it's messy. And Daniel… when something's off, tell me sooner, not later. I can handle the truth. That's part of how I grow, too."

Daniel nodded. "Then that's what we'll keep doing. And I will do better about being honest with feedback earlier. I owe that to you."

In that moment, he felt the weight shift. Instead of carrying it alone, he realized they were running this race side by side.

19

#5 Unafraid- The Baton of Courage and Vulnerability

Daniel decided to text John about what transpired with Kara.

"I feel dumb for having just told Kara what my boss said. Maybe I shouldn't have. I keep worrying it looks like I made a mistake… or worse, that she will see me as weak."

He hit send before he could overthink it. A few minutes later, his phone buzzed with a response from John.

"Notebook. U = Unafraid."

Another message from John followed immediately:

"You practiced vulnerability today. That's not weakness, that's part of being courageous. Call me in 15. Let's talk."

Daniel waited, the Critic whispering louder the longer the silence stretched: *"See? He doesn't even have time for you. He has more important things to do. Weak."*

But when the fifteen minutes were up, Daniel dialed John's number.

"Glad you called," John said as soon as he picked up. "Tell me what's circling your mind."

Daniel let out a shaky laugh. "The review rattled me. I thought I was making progress. The results say we are winning just as much as when I was doing it all myself, but then my boss made it sound like I've been slipping.

And I... admitted to Kara both what the boss said and that I am questioning my new approach. Now I'm second-guessing if that was the dumbest thing I could have done."

John's voice was steady. "Daniel, that wasn't dumb. That was courage. You trusted her with your honesty. That's not weakness, it's leadership."

"It didn't feel like leadership," Daniel muttered. "It felt like I was handing her proof I'm not good enough."

"That's the Critic talking," John said firmly. Then his voice grew quiet. "You know why I push this so hard? Because I used to do the opposite. I stayed silent when I should have spoken. "Once, in a leadership meeting, I knew the numbers we were celebrating were unsustainable. I bit my tongue because I didn't want to look like the guy throwing cold water to dampen everyone's joy. Months later, the bubble burst. Clients left. People lost jobs. But what cut deepest wasn't the revenue loss — it was the look in my team's eyes. They asked, 'Did you see this coming?' And I had to admit I had. My silence cost me their trust. Fear kept me quiet, and that silence broke more people than the sliding numbers. It broke people's faith in me. That wasn't strength, that was cowardice dressed as playing it safe."

"And at home?" John sighed. "For years, I dodged hard conversations with Mary. I thought keeping quiet kept the peace. Truth? The silence only built walls. It wasn't until I risked saying, 'You might be right, I might be failing us,' that we actually grew close again. Vulnerability looked like weakness to me. But it was the only path to trust."

Then John added, "That's why there is a U in GENUINE: Unafraid. Courage with vulnerability."

John went on, "We do the hard things, take calculated risks, and have tough conversations even when it's risky, messy, or uncertain, and sometimes that means we have to admit we messed up or don't know things."

Then Daniel asked, "So being unafraid doesn't mean nothing shakes me. It means choosing to be open, even when I feel shaky."

"Exactly," John said. "And people don't respect perfection. They respect leaders who are real enough to admit their limits and still keep moving. That's what Kara saw today. That's what she'll remember."

Daniel exhaled, running a thumb over the inked letters. "Then maybe… maybe I didn't blow it after all."

"No," John said warmly. "You didn't blow it. You picked up the next baton."

"Daniel," John continued, "the world says leaders can't show doubt. That courage is charging in with confidence, even when they know it's not accurate. But that's bravado, not bravery. Sometimes real courage means risking honesty when silence feels safer. Vulnerability isn't weakness; it's the deepest kind of strength. Because when you risk being real, you permit others to do the same."

John let the silence breathe on the line, then said, "Daniel, there's another part of being unafraid we need to talk about. Vulnerability is the start. But courage doesn't just flow downhill."

Daniel frowned, "What do you mean?"

"You were unafraid to admit doubt to Kara. Good. But the job isn't finished yet. Your boss needs to hear the same courage. You don't have to accept his perspective as truth. If you don't believe you're slipping because you've empowered Kara, tell him you disagree."

Daniel's chest tightened. "Disagreeing with him? That's… career suicide."

"No," John said firmly, "That's leadership. If, as a leader, you're the only one capable, you actually limit what the team can do. When you enable others to step up, you multiply impact. That's what your boss needs to learn. Yes, it's risky. And yes, Kara will fail at something at some point. But that's not a loss— it's an opportunity for you to teach her and for her to grow."

Daniel leaned back in his chair, staring at the ceiling. The Critic's whisper hissed: *"Don't do it. Play it safe. Keep your head down."*

John's voice cut through. "Being unafraid isn't about never feeling nervous. It's about not letting fear dictate what you do. You've already started. Now carry it through. Tell your boss the truth: Your job isn't to do it all yourself— it's to build a team that can do more than you ever could alone."

Daniel swallowed hard, gripping the phone tighter. "That sounds… bigger than anything I've tried before."

"That's because it is," John replied gently. "But Daniel, the baton doesn't get lighter as the race goes on. It gets heavier. And still, you carry it. This is the next stride. Do you have your notebook handy so I can share the anchors with you?"

Daniel affirmed with a "I sure do."

So, John got started.

The Anchors of Being Unafraid

Anchor #1. Name the Fear with Honesty and Frame It Toward Solutions

John's voice was steady. "Fear grows in silence. I used to walk into meetings terrified of being out of my depth, but I'd smile like I owned the room. You know what that did? It locked me inside my own head. I spent all my energy managing my perception instead of making meaningful contributions."

John continued, "One day, after a disastrous presentation, a colleague pulled me aside. She said, 'John, if you'd just said you didn't have the answer, we could've figured it out together. Instead, you froze, and we lost credibility.' That stung. I thought fear made me look weak. But hiding it made me weaker."

Daniel thought of his review with his boss—the suffocating silence, the vague, safe words he'd muttered. What if he had simply named the fear? I feel like I'm being measured by visibility, not by what I'm building. Naming it might have disarmed the Critic sooner.

John continued, "Let's get these anchors down in your notebook. Write the following:

Anchor #1: Name the fear with honesty and frame it toward solutions. Say what's true first. Naming fear shrinks it and invites help. When possible, share a reasonable next step or rationale for the truth.

Work — Examples:

- In a meeting, say, 'I don't have that number yet; here's what I do know, and here is my next step by 3 pm.'

- Tell your manager, 'I'm concerned we're being too positive on our outlook. Can we revisit the numbers before we share them broadly?'
- Tell your team, 'I'm stretched thin and might miss details. I need one of you to be my checker.'

Home — Example Scripts:

- 'I'm anxious about money; can we look at the budget together on Friday?'
- 'I'm distracted tonight; I want to be present. Can we take a walk so I can reset?'
- I'm afraid I'll disappoint you if I say no, but now isn't a great time for me. Can we plan another time that works?'

And try this Micro-action: In your next tense moment, think through one clean sentence: Here's what I'm afraid of: _____. Here's the next step: ____."

Anchor #2. Have the Hard Conversation Directly and ASAP

John leaned back. "I once avoided a tough talk with a direct report for six months. She was missing deadlines, team morale was cratering, but I kept putting it off—telling myself it would get better. By the time I finally sat down with her, resentment had spread like wildfire. The 30-minute conversation I avoided cost my team dozens of hours of rework."

Then John explained, "That's when I learned that silence feels safer, but it always costs more. Courage isn't confrontation—it's candor with truth delivered with the intent to build, not break the other person. When you tell the truth, even if it stings, you give someone the dignity of clarity and the opportunity to choose to change."

Daniel swallowed. He thought of Kara. If he had hidden after his review, she would have carried his silence as distance. Instead, by risking honesty, he discovered she respected him more. The conversation was hard, but silence would have been worse.

John went on, "Here's your next anchor to write down: Anchor #2: Have the hard conversation directly and ASAP. Speak the truth early, cleanly, and with care. Clarity is kindness. Speed is strength.

Work — Examples:

- Script: 'I respect you, and I need to say this clearly: When you_____. The impact is _____. I want to help—here's what support looks like.'
- Use the 4E approach in every hard talk. Evidence (what I saw you do-behavior) + effect (what the impact of what you did was) + expectation (what better would look like) in every hard talk. The fourth E is self-esteem. Make sure to share the feedback in a way that values the person.
- Schedule the conversation within 48 hours of recognizing the issue, but allow the person to reschedule the meeting once (feedback needs to be delivered when the other person can receive it).

Home — Examples:

- Admit when you are falling below the standard. 'I've been short with you and the kids. The impact is tension. I'm sorry. I'm asking for a reset tonight.'
- Acknowledge when things are changing and may impact others. 'When you change plans at the last minute, I feel spun. Can we agree to confirm by 4 pm?'
- Ask for help when you can't do what you say you will. 'I promised too much. I need to renegotiate Saturday, so I can keep my word on Sunday.'

And here's a good micro-action for you: Put a 15-minute block on your calendar to script one hard conversation using the 4E framework. Book it within two days. Have it. Follow up in a couple of days."

Anchor #3. Take the Right Risk

John's tone grew sharper. "It's not all about being vulnerable; being unafraid also involves doing hard things, but don't confuse unafraid with reckless. Years ago, I leapt into a partnership that looked glamorous—big names, shiny promises. I didn't ask the right questions, and I didn't slow down. I just wanted to look bold. Six months later, we were bleeding money and credibility. That wasn't courage. That was vanity in disguise."

Then John added, "Real courage asks: 'Is this risk aligned with my values/strategy? Will it grow people, not just my profit?' I had to learn to take the risks that stretched me in the right direction. Like saying no to a client request that would have made me money, but it would have cost the company far more than it was worth. Scary? Yes. But it showed I cared more about the combined team and our future than my own scoreboard."

Daniel realized his risk with Kara, letting her lead the client call was exactly that kind of courage. His boss saw weakness, but John was right. It wasn't about abdicating responsibility. It was about multiplying capacity. The client now knows he has a team, not just Daniel.

John went on, "So here's anchor #3 to write down: Take the right risks. Values-aligned, growth-focused, calculated risks. Bold ≠ reckless; bold = intentionally pushing beyond the boundary.

Work — Examples:

- Let a rising teammate lead the meeting; you play spotter and share credit.
- Disagree respectfully, with evidence, and frame it around shared goals. Even up the hierarchy when staying the course or changing direction could cause harm.
- Pilot a new process when it is a 'minimal viable product with a few loose ends' with one team for two to get feedback weeks before scaling.

Home — Examples:

- Say no to a good opportunity that would cost a critical family moment.
- Find an opportunity to get out of your comfort zone through a volunteer effort or engaging with different people than you typically do.
- Trust your spouse, child, or close friend to take on a set of responsibilities end-to-end, your way not required.

And try this micro-action: Write about one intentional risk you'll take this week (work or home), and how it aligns to a value. Share it with the person affected."

Anchor #4. Ask for Help or Forgiveness

John's voice softened. "This last anchor is hardest for me. For years, I thought leaders never apologized. Never admitted weakness. Mary once told me, 'You act like you have to hold everything up. But do you know how heavy it feels to live with someone who won't admit he needs me?' That one undid me."

John continued, "The first time I asked for forgiveness, really asked, it didn't shrink me. It built a bridge. Same at work. The day I admitted to my team I'd dropped the ball on a deliverable and asked them to help me fix it, the room changed. They leaned in instead of checking out. Because people trust leaders who bleed a little, not ones who pretend they're bulletproof."

Daniel felt that knot in his stomach again—remembering Rachel's quiet forgiveness when he owned up to being late for dinner, again. The Critic had called it a weakness. But with John's guidance, he saw it clearly: Asking for forgiveness wasn't shrinking. It was fearless love.

John went on, "So here's anchor #4: Ask for Help or Forgiveness. Own it early. Ask clearly. Receive help. Repair fast.

Work — Examples:

- A clean apology says, 'I did _____. Impact: _____. I'm sorry. Next time I'll _____.'

- Ask, 'I'm underwater on ____. Can you take A and B? I'll own C and debrief on Friday.'
- After repair, send a note to leadership naming the team's lift (credit outward).

Home — Examples:

- Apologize/ask for help with specifics and an action plan. 'I missed bedtime. I'm sorry. I'll block Wednesdays so it doesn't happen next week.'
- Apologize/ask for help and offer an alternative. 'I know I said I would do the drop off on Tuesday, but something came up; can I do it on Wednesday instead?'
- Apologize/ask for help by recognizing when someone covers your shortfall. 'Thank you for covering last night. I noticed—and I'm grateful.'

And here's a micro-action to do today: Make one clean apology or ask for one specific help. No explaining away. Full stop."

Daniel glanced down at the notebook again. "Courage with vulnerability," he read quietly. Then, more to himself than John, "And courage to stand up for what I know leadership really is."

"That's it," John said, his tone warm and steady. "Now you're running unafraid."

Applying Courage with the Boss

The next morning, Daniel stood outside his boss's office, the Critic already whispering. *"Don't do it. Say nothing. Just nod and survive."*

He drew a breath, straightened his shoulders, and stepped inside.

"Daniel," his boss said, glancing up from a stack of reports, "good to see you. I hope yesterday's review didn't discourage you too much."

Daniel managed a small smile. "It gave me a lot to think about." He hesitated for half a second, then remembered John's words: 'If you're the only one capable, you limit what can be done.' He leaned forward. "I'd like to revisit something you said."

The boss arched an eyebrow. "Oh?"

"You mentioned the perception that I'm slipping because Kara has been doing more, and I've been less directly available." Daniel clasped his hands together, steadying them. "I don't see it that way. I haven't been slipping. I've been leading intentionally, differently—by equipping Kara to step up. My job isn't to do everything. It's to build capacity, so the team can do more than I could ever accomplish alone."

The boss's expression didn't change. The Critic screamed: *"You've gone too far. Back down now."*

But Daniel pressed on. "Yes, it's risky. Kara might stumble. But that's when I coach her, and she grows. If I don't give her those chances, the organization never scales. Leadership that clings to control limits growth. Leadership that takes risks—creates it."

For a long moment, the room was quiet. Daniel felt the thump of his own heartbeat in his throat.

Finally, his boss leaned back in his chair, eyes narrowing slightly. Then—he nodded. "That's… a bold perspective. Risky, like you said."

Daniel forced himself not to flinch. "It is. But it's the right one."

Another pause. Then the boss gave a short laugh. "Well. I didn't expect you to push back. I'll admit—there's merit in what you're saying. Kara has impressed me. Maybe your approach deserves more credit than I gave it yesterday."

The Critic shrank, sputtering into silence.

Daniel let out a slow breath he hadn't realized he was holding. "Thank you," he said.

As he left the office, his phone buzzed—a text from John. "How'd it go?"

Daniel smiled, thumbs flying across the screen. "Still nervous. But I told him the truth. I didn't back down."

The reply came almost instantly: "Good. That's Unafraid."

This change didn't just feel like a new word to remember; it felt like a new way he was choosing to run.

Another buzz followed: "Fear runs in isolation. Courage passes the baton. You're not running solo anymore."

Daniel read the text twice. He realized he wasn't just carrying courage for himself; he was carrying it so others could run further, too.

Attempting Courage at Home

Despite that small victory, Daniel almost immediately fell short again the next morning. The kitchen buzzed with the noise of cereal bowls and clattering spoons. Daniel, still carrying last night's relief, tried to rush through breakfast before a call. When the kids started bickering over who would get the last pancake, his patience snapped.

"Enough!" he barked, louder than he meant. The room froze. His kids stared at him, wide-eyed, while the Critic's voice whispered: *"So much for growth. Some leader you are."*

Daniel carried the guilt with him through the rest of his morning routine. He came back to clear his mug, and the kids were still at the table, subdued. He took a breath, sat down, and forced himself to face them.

"Hey," he said quietly. "I need to tell you something. I shouldn't have yelled like that. I was wrong. Will you forgive me?"

The tension cracked. One of them shrugged, another grinned, and they nodded together. "It's okay, Dad. We forgive you."

The knot in his chest loosened again. The Critic had told him that courage was about never showing weakness. But here, at the breakfast table, courage was admitting fault. And that drew him closer to his kids than any show of strength ever could.

As Rachel was washing the charcoal off her hands from sketching earlier that morning, she turned just enough to meet Daniel's eyes, giving the faintest smile, quiet but proud. In that moment, Daniel realized his apology hadn't just restored something with his kids. It had strengthened something with her, too.

Later that night, upstairs, Daniel pulled out his phone and tapped a message: "John, I realized something today. Being unafraid is scary but rewarding."

He hit send. Almost immediately, the phone showed "Delivered", but John's Do Not Disturb mode was on.

Daniel smiled faintly, sliding the phone onto the nightstand. For once, he didn't need the instant reply. He already knew what John would say.

20

#6 Non-judgmental- The Baton of Curiosity

The buzz of Daniel's phone stirred him awake before dawn.

For a moment, he thought maybe John had lifted his Do Not Disturb and sent a word of encouragement after last night's texts. He fumbled for the screen, still half-asleep.

But the name wasn't John's.

It was Mark.

The text was longer than usual. No emojis. No photos.

"Got home last night. Empty house. She took our son. Just left a note saying, 'I guess we aren't enough. I hope everything else has been worth it.' I don't even know who else to tell."

Daniel blinked hard, completely unprepared for this type of heaviness first thing in the morning.

A harsh response from the Critic rose quickly: *"What did you expect, Mark? You've been running headfirst into this for years. You made this bed—now you're lying in it."*

Memories of Mark's one-liners flooded back:

- "Look, you've got to decide—are you playing for comfort or scale? I travel 200 days a year. That's the grind."

- "Don't feel guilty about missing bedtime stories, man. Kids don't remember that. They remember the big vacations."
- "Work hard, play harder."

The Critic's voice piled on: *"Say it. Call him out. He deserves it."*

But then the door burst open, and his daughter tumbled in, full of laughter. She launched herself onto the bed, giggling as she burrowed into the covers. The sharpness eased. Daniel let the phone fall onto the blanket and pulled her close. For a moment, the reply could wait.

Later that morning, Daniel spotted John at a corner booth in the café. Mary sat across from him with her hands wrapped around a mug of tea.

"Daniel," John said, waving him over. "Imagine seeing you here! Sit with us."

Daniel slid into the booth, still unsettled. John studied his face.

"You look like you didn't sleep."

Daniel sighed. "Mark texted me pretty early. His wife left. Took their son. Left a note saying he'd chosen everything else over them. And I'll be honest, part of me wanted to unload on him. He's been bragging for years about ignoring them for the grind. Feels like he finally got what was coming."

Mary's eyes softened. John leaned back, exhaling. "Daniel... I know that temptation. But I was once Mark."

Daniel blinked. "You?"

John nodded slowly. "Every bit of him. The grind, the bravado, the belief that if I just outpaced everyone else, I'd be winning. I had my definition of victory: Bigger titles, bigger numbers, more recognition. And by those standards, I was winning BIG. But here's the thing: No one else around me shared that definition. Not Mary. Not my kids. Not my closest friends. And because I never asked, because I wasn't curious, I never realized I was running the race at a pace no one else signed up for nor needed."

Mary leaned forward. "Daniel, he really believed he was winning. He'd point to the bank account, the travel schedule, the applause from his colleagues. But at home? We weren't applauding. We were exhausted. Lonely. Invisible."

John's voice broke a little. "One night, I came home to silence. Bags gone. Kids gone. Mary's note on the counter. That was my oh, shoot moment. And I realized—what's the point of breaking the finish line tape first if you're crossing the finish line all by yourself?"

Daniel sat still. The café sounds hummed in the background.

Mary placed her hand on John's. "The hardest thing wasn't his pace. It was his lack of engagement and curiosity. He never stopped to ask: 'What does winning look like for us?' He assumed his version was universal. That's the trap. When you don't ask, you assume. And when you assume, you don't notice you're winning a race no one else is excited about."

John nodded. "That's what I want you to hear, Daniel. There are two different ways to set your pace. One pace is set for more- more money, more status, more control. It's endless. The finish line keeps moving. The other pace is set for purpose- where you build the wins together and develop relationships. The trophy isn't bigger numbers or bank accounts. Instead, the result is deeper trust, shared joy, and people who want to run beside you. And what I found out is that purpose doesn't have to mean losing by other standards; it just means you achieve those wins differently.

Mary leaned in. "That's where non-judgment comes in. When I confronted John, it wasn't condemnation that changed him. It was curiosity. I asked him, 'Why are you running so hard? What are you afraid will happen if you slow down?' Judgment would have pushed him farther away. Curiosity pulled him back."

John looked Daniel square in the eye. "Your friend Mark doesn't need your preaching right now. He knows he's just been dealt a potentially fatal blow. What he needs is someone who believes he is worth attention in his weakest moment. A person who believes he can pick up the race at a different pace. And you get to decide, do you close the door with judgment, or open it with curiosity?"

Mary leaned in. "Here's what that means, Daniel: Non-Judgmental is choosing curiosity over condemnation. It's believing people are more than the sum of their worst choices or current status and giving them space to change instead of trapping them in a verdict. We can choose not to judge people for where they are on the journey and instead to support them towards where they are going."

John added, "It's not ignoring consequences. Mark has real consequences. But if you judge him, you shut the door on the belief that he can get to a better place. If you ask questions like, "What happened? Where are you? What do you need?" You leave room for him to walk through a new door and invite you to help him move forward."

The Cultural Objection

Daniel frowned. "But isn't judgment how we keep standards? Everywhere we look—social media, sports, schools, even at work—people act like the only way to make others change is to call them out. And honestly… a lot of it feels like fear. If you let things slide or even ask questions, doesn't that make you look weak or unsure? And if you don't instantly correct bad behavior or condemn the 'wrong' opinions, won't people assume you agree with them—or worse, turn on you?"

John nodded gently. "That's the stance a lot of people have, isn't it? We think judgment equals accountability. We think toughness means standing firm on our assumptions, so no one sees our uncertainty. Judgment feels safer because it puts us in control. Fear convinces us that if we don't judge quickly, we might be the next one judged."

Daniel raised an eyebrow. "So what you're telling me is being judgmental is actually just a form of being afraid?" He cracked a small grin. "That doesn't sound very GENUINE."

John laughed. "Exactly. Judgment hides fear behind confidence. Curiosity does the opposite—it takes courage. Judgment freezes people in their worst moments. Curiosity frees them to take the next step. Judgment says, 'This is who you are.' Curiosity asks, 'Who can you become?'"

Four Anchors of Being Non-Judgmental

Anchor #1. Eliminate Verdicts

John explained, "I once judged a colleague lazy because he missed a deadline. Months later, I learned his mother was dying. My verdict crushed trust before I even knew the full story. That's what judgment does, it closes the book on people too early."

Then Mary added, "And sometimes the verdict is silent but just as sharp. When John was in his grind years, I had already decided in my heart that he would never change. Every time I looked at him, that judgment leaked out. He could feel it. The night I left the note, I realized my verdict had become his cage. It wasn't until I suspended it, until I stopped predicting failure, that he even had space to try."

Daniel took out his notebook that he now always carried with him, and John smiled and said, "I'm so glad you have that, now let's write this all down…

Here's anchor #1: Eliminate Verdicts. Delay conclusions. Assume there's more to the story than what you can see.

Work — Examples:

- Use the No Label Without Context rule; before labeling a behavior, investigate context first.
- Swap attribution (lazy, checked out) for observation: 'You missed the Tuesday deadline.'
- Ask for two data points you don't have before you form an opinion.

Home — Examples:

- When you mess up, pause and reflect to yourself, 'The story I'm telling myself is ____. What else might be true?'
- Pause before global labels/hyperbole ('you never…'). Describe the moment instead.
- With kids, say, 'What made today hard?' before giving advice.

And here's a good micro-action: When you make a mistake this week, write: 'The story I'm telling myself is ____.' Then add one alternative story that could also be true (and at least a bit more positive)."

Anchor #2. Ask Questions

John began, "The turning point for me came when Mary didn't accuse me, but asked me: 'Why are you running so hard? What are you afraid will happen if you stop?' That question unraveled me. Judgment always made me defensive. But her curiosity broke through my armor."

Then Mary continued, "Questions create space. Accusations close it. When I asked instead of accusing him, John didn't fight me; he let me in. In the classroom, it's the same. If a student lashes out and I ask, 'What's going on?' instead of 'Why are you being difficult?' they usually tell me the truth. Curiosity opens doors, judgment slams them shut. But don't assume they are going to run through the door. It takes time to get comfortable with curiosity because we are all so used to being judged. Allow space for that too."

Then John chimed in, "Let's add anchor #2: Ask questions. Lead with three honest questions before giving an opinion.

Work — Examples:

- 3Q rule in 1:1s: 'What outcome are you aiming at? Where are you stuck? What do you think caused you to get stuck?' Then make a statement based on deeper knowledge.
- In conflict, try, 'What did you hear me say? What did you hope I'd say?'
- In post-mortems, ask, 'What surprised you? What would you try differently next time?"

Home — Examples:

- With your spouse, create space for learning by saying, 'What felt heaviest

today? What felt hopeful?'
- With kids, you can ask, 'On a scale of 1–10, where are you right now? What would move you to one higher number?'
- Family planning, offer this question, 'What would good look like for you this weekend?'

And here's a micro-action to challenge you today: Replace your first opinion with one curious question. Let the other person talk twice as long as you."

Anchor #3. Separate Person from Problem

John went on, "I used to combine a person's identity with their mistakes. If someone dropped the ball, I'd label them unreliable. When I made mistakes, I labeled myself a failure. That shame poisoned relationships. It wasn't until I learned to say, 'You failed here, but you are not a failure,' that people started to trust me again."

Then Mary added, "I had to learn that, too. When I confronted John, it was tempting to say, 'You are selfish.' But I realized what I needed to name was the behavior, not his whole being. 'You're working in a way that makes us invisible.' That's different than saying, 'You are a bad husband.' The first example opens the door to change. The second chains someone to condemnation."

John continued, "So that leads us to anchor #3. Separate the person from the problem. Name the behavior and impact—without naming the person.

Work — Examples:

- Use the 4E framework: Evidence ('We missed Tuesday's handoff"), Effect ('The client lost confidence'), Expectation ('We'll confirm by noon the day before'), Self-Esteem (add a comment about belief in the person and future growth: 'This miss doesn't define you. I know you can nail the next one.')
- Don't participate in the meeting after the meeting or communicate

about others in the meeting behind their back. This is damaging and disrespectful if you aren't willing to say the thing out loud in front of others; don't silently type it.

- Focus more on future growth than current status. Take the time to understand why people do what they do, rather than focus on why it was wrong.

Home — Examples:

- With your spouse/significant other, you can say, 'When we change plans at the last minute, I feel thrown off. Can we confirm by 4 pm?'
- With kids, explain, 'Throwing the toy is not okay. You're not bad—you're mad. Let's try words.'
- With yourself, think, 'I made a mistake,' instead of 'I am a mistake.'

Here's a good micro-action for you: The next time you are going to label a person based on something they did, take that 'you are' sentence and rewrite it as behavior → impact → request. So instead of 'you are so stupid,' say, 'When you didn't double check the amount, the check you sent was wrong. Next time, double-check the amount before you send the check.'"

Anchor #4. Believe in Possibility

John shared, "I had mentors who gave up on me, said I'd never slow down, never change. I lived into that judgment for years. Then Mary said the opposite: 'I still believe you can be the man I married. I believe you can lead differently.' That belief gave me the courage to actually try."

Mary continued, "Believing in possibility is a choice, not a feeling. Honestly, I didn't feel hopeful when I said those words to John. But I chose them anyway. Judgment says, 'You'll always be this way.' Belief says, 'You're not finished yet.' And sometimes, someone else's belief is what carries you when you can't carry yourself."

Daniel felt the truth of it—how a single sentence could make room to change.

John continued, "So, here's anchor #4: Believe in possibility. Believe a better future is possible for people and say it out loud.

Work — Examples:

- Say, 'I believe you can own this client by Q4; here's the support and the guardrails.'
- Offer a second chance with clear conditions and coaching.
- Keep a progress log with clear next steps and goals so you can celebrate growth you've actually seen.

Home — Examples:

- Say, 'I see you becoming more patient with your sister—keep going.'
- Offer this encouragement, 'I believe we can rebuild this, one honest week at a time.'
- Tell a child, 'You're learning to be brave. I can see it when you _____.'

And a micro-action for you to try: Send a belief note (three sentences) to one person: Who they're becoming, one proof you've seen, one next step you'll support."

Framing for Daniel

John continued, "These are the anchors, Daniel. Eliminate verdicts. Ask questions. Separate the person from the problem. Believe in possibility. Judgment freezes people in their worst moments. Curiosity lets them take the next step."

Mary leaned in, her voice gentle. "When you choose curiosity, you're not excusing what happened. You're saying, 'You're more than this mistake, and I'll walk with you into what's next.' That's what Mark needs from you now. That's what Kara will need from you, too, as you continue to give her a chance to grow. Non-judgment isn't blind optimism. It's refusing to trap people in their worst chapter. It's saying: 'Your story isn't finished yet.'"

Daniel was still a bit uncertain. Maybe that was the gift he could give Mark—not excusing him but believing he wasn't condemned to stay at the bottom of the well. He would need Daniel's encouragement and belief that he could climb out of that well.

Daniel traced the letters with his finger. He looked back at his phone. Mark's message was still towards the top of his message list.

He took a breath and started typing.

"Mark, I am so sorry. That sounds heavy and unexpected. Where are you right now?"

He pressed send. No lecture. No verdict. Just curiosity.

John smiled after Daniel showed him his response. "That's it. You just handed him a chance to join you in running at a different pace."

Daniel grabbed his notebook like a relic worth keeping. By the time he left the coffee shop, he felt lighter, steadier. Maybe even ready to take on the day with full curiosity and focus on the possible, not the past. Halfway to the office, his phone buzzed again. It was Kara.

He answered cheerfully. "Hey—good timing. I was just about—"

Her voice cut him off, tight and rushed. "Daniel, I screwed up."

The bottom dropped out of his chest. "What happened?"

"I took the lead on that client call this morning—you know, the one we prepped for yesterday? I thought I could push them to commit. But I overstepped. Said things I shouldn't have promised. They're furious. They said they might walk."

Daniel gripped the wheel, heat rising in his chest. The Critic immediately attacked, *"What were you thinking, Kara? We went over this. You can't just freelance strategy like that."* The harsh words lined up, ready to fire.

But then—Mary's comments flashed in his mind. 'Non-Judgmental = choosing curiosity over condemnation.'

He forced himself to pause.

"Kara," he said slowly, "I can hear how rattled you are. Take a breath. Walk me through exactly what you said."

There was a beat of silence. Then she exhaled. "I... I told them we could cut the implementation time in half. I thought if I showed confidence, it would lock them in. But now they're saying if we can't deliver, they're pulling the deal."

Daniel closed his eyes. Harshness still pressed at the edges, but curiosity pushed it back. "Okay. You wanted to help us win. That tells me your heart was in the right place. Now, let's figure out how to repair this together."

Her voice wavered. "You're not... mad?"

"I'm not ready to label this as a loss," Daniel said firmly. "Mistakes happen. This wasn't the best way to handle the situation, but you already know that. Now it's more important we figure out where we go from here."

There was a pause. Then Kara's voice steadied. "I can call them back and own my mistake. Tell them I got ahead of myself and that leadership is recalibrating the plan."

"That's a start," Daniel said. "And I'll back you up. You don't have to fix this alone."

When the call ended, Daniel glanced at the notebook in his passenger seat. He just experienced how non-judgment wasn't just a nice idea. It was the difference between shame shutting someone down and curiosity calling them forward.

He knew that making this situation right would require him to stay later than expected this evening. He remembered his commitment to Rachel to communicate when his situation would change, and it would impact the family. So, he quickly pulled over and sent her a text. "Hey, Babe. Kara needs my help to fix a significant issue. I will be late tonight. I am sorry." Daniel hit send and tossed his phone in the seat next to the notebook.

When he got to the office, he grabbed his phone and saw a reply from Rachel. It was direct, but exactly what he needed to hear. "No problem. Thanks for following through and keeping me in the loop as we talked about. If things at work have shifted for the better, like the way they have here at home, I'm sure it will work out, and your team will rally. You have always been great in a crisis."

Daniel was both relieved and encouraged to see Rachel's response.

21

#7: Empathy- The Baton of Understanding

By lunchtime, the office was still humming with tension as the team worked to untangle the fallout from Kara's earlier mistake. No one was pointing fingers anymore; it wasn't about blame; it was about fixing things fast and moving forward.

Daniel spotted Chris at his desk, shuffling papers with jerky movements. He was clearly trying to stay locked in, but his eyes kept flicking toward the clock. Finally, Chris muttered under his breath and stood, running a hand through his hair.

Daniel walked over. "Hey, are you okay?"

Chris let out a sharp breath. "Honestly? I'm stretched thin. I want to help pull us through this, but I've got to leave soon. My wife is at the hospital with our son, and I'm already late getting there. I'm trying to be two places at once, and I feel like I'm not present in either."

The old Daniel might have zeroed in on the work, reminding Chris that the client needed things fixed tonight. But John and Mary's words from the morning still echoed: "Curiosity over criticism. Relationship over rebuke."

Daniel drew in a slow breath, noticed the strain on Chris's face, and said, "That's a lot to carry. Tell me what you're feeling right now."

There was silence, then a shaky exhale. "Scared. Frustrated. Rushed.

Like I let everyone down. I thought I was proving myself, but now I just feel... small."

Daniel nodded slowly and responded. "Your emotions are real. And they matter. It must be hard knowing your wife and son need you and feeling like work needs you too. But you don't have to carry it alone. Let's figure out what can be passed off so you can get to your family."

Chris's eyes flickered with relief. He nodded slowly. "Thanks. I didn't want to say anything, I didn't want to let anyone down."

"You're not letting anyone down," Daniel replied. "We'll rally as a team. You go be where you are needed most."

Naming the Baton

The team had rallied nicely, and as the end of the long day neared, Daniel sat at his desk, replaying the conversation with Chris. He wrote one word on a sticky note: Emotions.

He snapped a photo and texted it to John: "Think I've got the last one."

The reply came back almost instantly.

John: "Not quite. You're close, but it's more than just naming emotions."

Daniel frowned, waiting. Then another bubble appeared.

John texted again: "Empathy = Emotions are real and impact how we interact. Slow down to listen, see through their eyes, and feel what they feel before taking action."

Daniel stared at the words. He read them again, slower this time. "Feel what they feel before taking action."

He thought back to Kara's trembling voice on the phone. He could have scolded her. He almost had. But instead, he'd slowed down. Asked. Listened. And in that pause, her shame had softened into a desire to solve the problem together.

Daniel typed back: "So empathy is about creating that pause? Choosing to step into their shoes before stepping into a solution?"

John's dots bounced for a second. Then he responded, "Exactly. Empathy builds the bridge before you try to cross it. Without it, every correction feels like condemnation, and every emotion feels out of place."

Daniel leaned back in his chair. He could still feel Kara's relief over the phone when she realized he wasn't angry, and Chris's relief that he wasn't told how he felt was wrong or didn't matter. And now, seeing it in John's words, he recognized it: Empathy wasn't sappy. It was a strength that made a deep connection possible.

John sent another text summarizing Empathy, and Daniel grabbed his notebook and jotted that definition on a new page.

Empathy = Emotions are real and impact how we interact. Slow down to listen, see through their eyes, and feel what they feel before acting.

This time, he circled the words, "Before acting."

Putting It in Practice

As Daniel was getting ready to leave, Kara knocked lightly on his office door. Her eyes still held the weight of the morning and the tiredness of having worked hard to make it right, but there was a flicker of resolve, too.

"Do you have a minute?" she asked.

Daniel waved her in. "Of course. How are you holding up?"

She sighed. "Better. I've been thinking about what you said — slowing down, listening. I know I need to talk to my team, but honestly… I'm terrified. What if they've already written me off?"

Daniel leaned forward. "That's where empathy comes in. Don't start with fixing. Start with feeling. Walk into that room and name what they're probably feeling: Exhausted, frustrated, maybe even let down. Let them see you understand before you ask them to understand you."

Kara nodded slowly. "So, I don't defend. I don't explain. I just create space and… listen first."

"Exactly," Daniel said. "Empathy builds a bridge so you can more safely cross the divide between the situation and the reaction. If you honor what they feel, they'll be more open to what you offer as a potential path forward."

She exhaled, the fear loosening slightly. "Okay. I can do that."

Daniel smiled. "You already started this morning. You let me in on your embarrassment. Now give your team the same chance and then walk with them through it."

Kara straightened, almost visibly taller. "Thanks, Daniel. I needed this."

As she left, Daniel sat back in his chair. It sank in that empathy wasn't about indulging emotions; it was about giving people the dignity of being heard. Naming what Kara felt hadn't erased the problem, but it had changed the way they faced it together. Empathy wasn't a weakness. It was the discipline of building trust when pressure could have fractured it.

The Empathy Demonstration (John's Encounter)

That weekend, Daniel met John at their usual diner. The crowd was larger than usual. The café was filled with runners having just finished the community 5K race. John waved him over to a small table in the middle of the restaurant that was not nearly as private as their typical corner booth.

Before they could even order, a young man in his early twenties shuffled past their table, bumping John's shoulder. The man muttered something under his breath, his hoodie pulled tight, his face lined with exhaustion.

Daniel, weary from a long week at work, including the near all-nighter resolving the client matter, was thinking of how he would have snapped at the rude jerk who bumped into John. But John had a different reply.

"Hey," John said gently, leaning toward the young man, "rough morning?"

The man stopped, wary. "What's it to you?"

"Nothing," John shrugged. "Just looked like you've got more on your plate than the rest of us."

The young man hesitated. His posture softened. "Yeah... just got fired. Rent's due. I am scared that I'm running short of options."

Daniel watched closely. John didn't brush past the pain with a quick, "You'll be fine." He didn't tell him to bury it or pretend it didn't hurt. Instead, he let the weight sit in the air and nodded, slow and steady. "Man, that's heavy. I've been in a spot like that before. Feels like the whole world's stacked against you."

The young man blinked, as if being understood was the very thing he hadn't expected. "Exactly."

John slid a business card across the table. "I don't have all the answers, but I do know a guy who's hiring. And if you need a meal, this place will take care of it. Put it on my tab."

The man's eyes flickered with relief, the tension in his face softening. "Thanks. I... I didn't expect that."

"No problem," John said with a small smile. "We all need someone to see the weight we're carrying and give us options to share it if we choose."

When the young man left, Daniel leaned in. "You could've dismissed his struggle and told him to toughen up. But instead, you gave him space to feel it, and that changed everything."

John folded his hands and placed them on the table. "That's the thing, Daniel. Dismissiveness shuts people down — it ignores what they feel and pushes them to just move on. Empathy does the opposite. It slows down long enough to say, 'I get it, how you are feeling matters.' When I was younger, I thought the goal was to keep a poker face and never let emotions show. But that approach was exhausting for me and draining for everyone else. When I finally accepted that emotions are real and they shape how we interact, I discovered something better — the real win is creating space for feelings to breathe long enough that you can name them and then choose an informed way forward."

Daniel thought back to Kara's trembling voice and now this young man's raw honesty. Both moments carried the same theme. When empathy enters, walls fall.

John smiled, almost reading his thoughts. "Empathy isn't about rushing past emotions before they have room to breathe. It's the opposite of brushing people off or telling them to toughen up. Empathy means refusing to let someone stand alone in what they feel, and that's how we build bridges strong enough to carry the weight of real change."

The Cultural Objection

Daniel frowned. "But isn't empathy kind of... soft? Doesn't it slow you down? People don't want a shoulder to cry on. They want results."

John nodded. "That's the lie I believed: That emotions are distractions."

Daniel leaned back in his chair. "It's not just me, though. Everywhere you look, people talk like emotions are either a liability or a weapon. At work, if you share how you really feel, you're 'unprofessional' or 'too sensitive.' Online, if you admit you're struggling, someone tells you to toughen up or uses it against you later. Half the time it feels safer to shut down than open up."

He rubbed his forehead. "And on the other side, if you invite people to share what they're feeling, you're terrified you'll get stuck in a never-ending vent session. Or that they'll cry and you won't know what to say. Or they'll ask you for something you can't fix. So, everyone just keeps it surface level and calls it 'being efficient.'"

John's expression softened. "Exactly. We've trained ourselves to avoid emotions from both sides. People avoid sharing because they don't want to be labeled as weak, dramatic, or 'too much.' They've learned that being honest can get them criticized, corrected, or quietly avoided. So, they keep their real thoughts and feelings under lock and key and only show the version they think everyone will tolerate."

He continued, "And people avoid hearing emotions because they're afraid of being overwhelmed or obligated. They're scared that if they really listen, they'll have to fix it, or they'll say the wrong thing, or they'll feel more than they're comfortable feeling. So, they stay busy. They stay in their heads. They change the subject. They call it 'staying focused,' but really it's self-protection."

Daniel thought about his own patterns — how many times he'd cut off Rachel's emotions by jumping straight to solutions or changing the topic with his team when things got too raw. "So, when I dodge emotions, it's not just about being efficient. It's about being afraid I'll get pulled into something I can't control."

John nodded. "Right. And the culture around us reinforces it. We celebrate people who 'power through' and 'don't let feelings get in the way.' We rarely celebrate the person who slowed down long enough to really understand someone before making a decision. We've made toughness look like numbness, when real toughness is the courage to stay present when emotions show up."

Daniel let out a slow breath. "No wonder people keep everything bottled up. If they share, they risk being judged. If they listen, they risk being uncomfortable."

"That's the tension empathy speaks into," John said. "Empathy isn't about turning every meeting into group therapy. It's not about coddling or excusing unhealthy behavior. It's about refusing to pretend that emotions don't exist just because they're inconvenient. Emotions drive decisions. Ignore them, and you'll never understand why people act the way they do."

He paused, then added, "Empathy isn't about pity parties; it's about partnership. It says, 'Your feelings are real, and they're part of the story. Let's understand them so we can move forward wisely.' It's not about being sentimental or dismissing away behavior because of emotional reactions — it's about being smart enough to know that logic alone never moves the human heart."

He looked back up at John. "So, the real objection isn't that empathy is soft," he said slowly. "It's that it feels risky."

John smiled. "Exactly. Empathy feels risky because it's real. But that's also why it works."

Four Anchors of Empathy

Anchor #1. Name the Emotion

John leaned in. "Daniel, when I was younger, I thought emotions were distractions. If someone cried, I'd tell them to calm down or move on. All that did was push them deeper into shame. What I've learned is this: When you name what you see — 'You look frustrated,' or 'That sounds

155

disappointing' — people feel seen instead of silenced. That's the first move of empathy. Name the emotion out loud."

Daniel thought of moments when someone had said 'I'm fine,' but their hunched shoulders told a different story.

John continued, "Let's get this down in your notebook. Add Anchor #1: Name the emotion. Name what you see/hear. Label the feeling without judging it.

Work — Examples:

- Ask the person to use an emotion word so you hear it straight from them. 'What are you feeling right now?'
- If you notice something brewing, it is okay to include the emotion in your description, because sometimes we misinterpret. 'I'm hearing frustration over the tight timeline—does that match what you are feeling?'
- Reinforce that emotions are natural and okay to experience. 'That was a punch in the gut, right? It makes sense to take a minute before pushing past.'

Home — Examples:

- Ask, 'You seem tense—tough day?'
- Respond with, 'That sounded embarrassing. I'd feel that, too.'
- Reply to kids, 'Looks like you're mad and a little sad.'

And try this micro-action: In your next conversation, begin with one feeling label: 'Sounds like you're ____.'"

Anchor #2. Sit in the Pause

John took a sip of his coffee, his tone quieter now. "I used to think silence was weakness, like I didn't know what to do to help. Whenever someone got emotional, I filled the space with fixes or explanations. But sometimes, the most powerful thing you can do is sit in the pause. Years ago, a teammate told me he'd lost his father. I froze. I didn't know what to say, so I just sat with him. Ten minutes passed in silence. Later, he told me it was the most supportive thing anyone had done. Empathy means you don't rush to fill the air. You let presence speak first."

He smiled sadly. "Silence isn't weakness. It's space for the other person to breathe. Now write down Anchor #2: Sit in the pause. Hold the moment. Don't rush to patch it up.

Work — Examples:

- After hard news, count to eight in your head before speaking.
- Use a simple bridge: 'I'm here,' then pause.
- Don't be afraid to create extra space by inviting them to take a walk and revisit the conversation later.

Home — Examples:

- Sit shoulder-to-shoulder for a minute before talking.
- Offer a hand, not a plan: 'Want a hug or some quiet?'
- At dinner, if someone shares a hard thing, let the table breathe.

Here's a good micro-action: Practice the eight-second pause before you share a reaction during an emotional exchange ."

Anchor #3. Stay Focused on Their Experience

John tapped the notebook with his pen. "Most of the time, we jump to share and compare: 'That happened to me once too…' We think it builds connection, but really, it shifts the spotlight back to us. Empathy says: Keep the focus on them. Stay in their story, not yours. That keeps their emotions at the center instead of turning it into a comparison contest."

He leaned forward. "I once had a teammate drop the ball on a big deadline. My instinct was to tell him about the time I dropped the ball in a similar situation. But instead, I asked, 'What was the hardest part for you in this project?' His answer showed me things I hadn't seen — late nights, family struggles, roadblocks he hadn't voiced. By staying in his perspective instead of shifting to mine, the conversation became about trust, not competition."

John added, "There may be a time to share your story, but not until theirs has been fully heard. Empathy listens first, then carefully decides if your experience will help, not hijack, the moment."

Daniel nodded slowly, the truth of it sinking in. He could recall moments when someone had rushed to say, "That happened to me too," and how it always left him feeling smaller, like his own struggle was just a footnote to their story. But the rare times when someone had stayed with his experience — letting him lead, asking follow-up questions, sitting in the tension without redirecting — those were the times he'd walked away lighter, not lonelier. He realized now how easy it was to shift the spotlight without intending to, and how much discipline it took to resist it. Empathy, he thought, wasn't about finding common ground through comparison. It was about giving the other person the dignity of being center stage until they were ready to hand it back.

John continued, "Let's dive into Anchor #3: Stay focused on their experience. Keep the focus on their experience, not your comparison.

Work — Examples:

- Instead of saying, 'That happened to me too,' try asking, 'What part of this felt hardest for you?'

- When someone vents, resist giving your story. Instead, say, 'Tell me more about how that felt for you.'
- In debriefs, use: 'What's one thing you wish I understood better about what you went through?'

Home — Examples:

- With kids: Instead of saying, 'I went through that too at your age', try, 'What does it feel like for you right now?'
- With your spouse, say, 'I want to understand how that felt for you,' before offering your perspective.
- At the dinner table, ask one person to share their highlight or hardest moment, and just listen without adding your own.

Here's a micro-action for today: In your next conversation, resist the urge to say, 'That happened to me too.' Instead, ask one follow-up that keeps the focus on their experience."

Anchor #4. Feel Before You Fix

John sat back, voice steady. "This next anchor is the hardest for me, Daniel. Leaders are wired to fix. We see a problem, and we rush to patch it, repair it, and map out the next steps. But empathy says: Feel it first. If you skip the feeling, the fix rarely lands."

He shook his head, remembering. "I once had a team member lose a major client account. My instinct was to grab the whiteboard and start listing recovery strategies. But I caught myself. Instead, I paused and simply said, 'How are you feeling right now?' His shoulders dropped. The tension left his face. He shared his feelings of personal disappointment and fear that it would cost him his job. After feeling understood, he was ready to fully engage in moving forward to solve the situation. I learned that day that empathy isn't about abandoning action; it's about sequencing. Connection before correction. Feel before you fix."

He leaned forward. "And here's the trap I had to unlearn: We think acknowledging emotions will slow everything down. But the truth? It speeds up trust. A solution offered too soon feels like control. A solution given after empathy feels like support."

Daniel winced, the memory of his own mistake surfacing. "I've blown that," he admitted. "Last quarter, when Kara expressed how overwhelmed she was on the client rollout, I cut her off with, 'Okay, here's what we'll do—let's reassign two tasks and extend the timeline.' I thought I was being efficient. But she went quiet, and later I heard from Mike that she felt like I didn't even care she was drowning. I gave her a fix, but I didn't give her space to breathe first. That fix just made her feel more invisible."

John nodded gently. "Exactly. The right answer, delivered without empathy, still misses the mark. People don't just need direction — they need to know you notice their pain. That's what makes your solutions stick. Let's write down Anchor #4: Feel before you fix. Anchor: Acknowledge → Validate → Ask. Then collaborate.

Work — Examples:

- Acknowledge by saying, 'I bet this hurts.'
- Validate with, 'It makes sense you're upset.'
- Ask, 'Do you want support or a solution first?'
- Then: Co-design next steps and owners.

Home — Examples:

- Acknowledge by saying, 'That was humiliating; I'd want to hide, too.'
- Validate with, 'Do you want me to sit with you, or help brainstorm?'
- Ask after feelings settle, 'What would help the most tonight?'
- Then: Co-design how you can be helpful in the healing.

And here's a great micro-action for you: Use the line: 'Do you want support or a solution?' Then follow their answer."

Closing the Empathy Baton

John concluded, "Those are the anchors, Daniel. Name the emotion. Sit in the pause. See through their eyes. Feel before you fix. Empathy isn't soft; it's strong enough to carry the weight of someone else's emotions, if only for a moment. It's having the courage to sit in a storm with someone else without feeling like you need to immediately grab an umbrella. And that strength builds trust faster than any lecture ever could."

Daniel got a quizzical look in his eyes and asked John a question, "With your race analogy, is it fair to say that empathy in relationships, sitting with people in their emotions, and helping them heal without getting stuck serves the same purpose as a sports trainer does for an athlete who is hurting during a race?"

John looked a little lost, but Daniel went further, "Empathy is about emotional healing, so without knowing the real feeling and cause, you can't treat it well. It would be like the sports trainer showing up to a runner in pain and starting to tape his ankle without asking what was hurting. You might be solving the wrong thing, which isn't going to help the person get back in the race faster."

Now John understood where he was going, and simply said, "Exactly. You shouldn't lead with the solution when someone shares their struggles with you. You need to start by helping them diagnose what they are really feeling and why they might be feeling that way."

With that, John got a little sentimental with Daniel, "This is the last baton, Daniel. It's not soft — it's the strength that keeps the relay connected. Without it, the handoff drops. With it, the race continues."

22

The Batons are Passed, but the Race Isn't Over

Daniel ran a thumb over the letters, realizing this wasn't just ink in a notebook anymore. One baton at a time, he was learning to run the race differently. He was being equipped to run relays instead of solo sprints and to win as a team, not just individually.

Daniel reflected on John's interaction with the young man who'd just lost his job. Daniel finally understood that these principles work for more than just work or home. So, he said, "All of these batons can positively impact any relationship, anywhere. Not just at work or at home." And John took a sip of his coffee and leaned back. "Daniel, that's the beauty of this. These principles — generosity, engagement, nice, unafraid, integrity, non-judgment, empathy — they aren't just for the office or your family. They're for life. Every person you meet, every conversation you step into, every interruption on the street, it's all ground to practice them. And they have the potential to positively impact all your interactions."

Daniel raised an eyebrow. "So, it's not about context. It's about consistency."

"Exactly," John said, his tone steady. "The mistake I made for years was thinking I could wear different masks. Professional John. Family John. Social John. But the truth is, that's exhausting, and it's hollow. Integrity means you live one life, not a collection of performances, and the other six batons are the principles for running differently that make it easier to be more consistent, consequently having better results for your life as a whole."

John continued, "Empathy with Kara in the office looked like slowing down and listening. Empathy with that young man who bumped me looked like offering dignity and a meal. Different setting. Same posture, just modifying the actions based on the situation. The GENUINE traits can be combined and modified as needed, as long as you have the integrity to remain true to their intent. Which is to positively impact the lives of the people around you and by doing so, improve your own life."

Daniel sat back, letting the weight of it sink in. The GENUINE traits weren't boxes to check depending on the situation; they were intentional ways to live your whole life.

23

The Check-In: Staying the Course

Smoke curled upward, carrying the smell of charred beef across the backyard. Kids' laughter echoed from the basketball hoop at the end of the driveway, punctuated by the rhythmic thud of a ball hitting pavement. Paul's wife stood chatting with a cluster of neighbors, her gift of hospitality on full display.

Paul, as usual, took his post at the grill, the one place he could stand, spatula in hand, feeling both useful and out of the spotlight. Hosting wasn't really his style, but over time, he'd realized honoring his wife's gift meant learning to play his role, too. The steady motion of flipping burgers felt like a contribution.

Out of the corner of his eye, he noticed Daniel standing a few feet away. His posture was tight, shoulders hunched slightly forward, face caught between a polite smile and something that seemed heavier. Paul asked a few customary niceties — "How you been? How are the kids? What did you think of the game last week?" — but Daniel's tone portrayed something deeper."

Paul decided to give him an opening. "John tells me you've been trying to run the race differently. How's it going?"

It had been a few months since Daniel had been implementing the GEN-UINE batons, and the adjustments weren't coming easily or consistently. He exhaled, a long, slow breath as if he'd been holding it all week. "Hard. Honestly, it is harder than I expected. I keep slipping back. Some days I nail it, other days, I feel like the old me all over again. People still give me these looks like I'm faking it. I know Rachel wants to believe in me, but I see her wondering if it'll stick. Was it like that for you?"

Paul smirked, flipping the spatula in his hand. "Worse. First week, I taped the list of batons to the office wall like it was a company vision statement. I told my employees, 'We're all going to run the GENUINE way from now on.' You should've seen their faces. Turns out you can't force transformation overnight."

Paul continued, "When John talks about non-judgmental, and how everyone is on a journey, and it impacts how they show up and react and treat others… He isn't kidding. People are just all so different. And even though running differently was working well for me, not everyone was willing to change everything about how they ran just based on my assurance of how much better it felt to run in a new way."

Then Paul explained, "Some people would pick and choose some of the principles. Like I had one guy who tried being more generous, helping the new guys learn the ropes, but he still refused to have the hard conversations about boundaries, so he ended up feeling worn out because people would always interrupt his lunch with questions."

Paul continued, "One lady tried being more empathetic with her son, who was struggling with his emotions when he broke up with his girlfriend, but she grew discouraged because when she would talk about an issue at work, her son would just stare at his phone and basically tell her to suck it up. She told me she was done because there was no point in running differently if everyone around her was just going to keep being the same."

Daniel cracked a smile, but his eyes stayed serious. "You haven't given it up yet?"

Paul leaned back, letting the hiss of the grill fill a pause. "No way, because when I get it right, the results are amazing. I just have to be willing to keep leaning into the process. That's the work, Daniel. Change isn't about flipping a switch. It's training muscles. You stumble, reset, repeat. But I'll tell you what helped me most — I built my change anchors with specific practices that keep me willing to take action when I don't like the immediate results I am getting."

Daniel tilted his head and grinned. "I am learning to love a good set of anchors."

They both chuckled. Paul grabbed a paper plate and the Sharpie he always kept tucked in his apron. "Here's how I learned to stay the course."

Four Anchors of Staying the Course

Anchor #1. Start Small, Start Daily

Paul set down the plate and wrote, Anchor #1: Start small, start daily. Then he explained, "My biggest mistake was thinking I could overhaul everything in a week. Real change doesn't work like that. Habits are built in reps, not resolutions. I had to start embarrassingly small. One action a day. At first, it felt trivial holding the door, putting my phone down for ten minutes. But it stacked."

Daniel nodded. "I think that's where I trip up. I try to sprint full speed ahead, but then I burn out."

"Exactly," Paul said. "Running the race differently isn't about heroic streaks. It's about daily reps. Let's add this to the plate. Anchor: Build daily reps, not heroic streaks.

Work Examples:

- Before every meeting, write down one person you want to affirm.
- Commit to one distraction-free 20-minute block every day.
- Use your travel time to plan your day with a commitment and end your day with a reflection.

Home Examples:

- Talk with someone (spouse/friend) about one GENUINE action/commitment every night.

- End the day by naming one thing you appreciated about your kids using GENUINE language.
- Commit to 15 mins of learning a day on one of the GENUINE principles.

And here's a good Micro-action to do: Choose one micro-action you can repeat daily for the next week."

Daniel smiled faintly. "So even if it feels small, it counts?"

Paul shrugged. "That's the only way anything ever grows. One small step at a time."

Anchor #2. Expect Resistance (Inside and Out)

Paul poked at the burgers, then turned back and wrote on the plate: Anchor #2: Expect resistance. "I thought my inner Critic would retire once I started changing. Nope — his voice just got louder and told me I was faking it; told me I'd never stick to it. And then there were the people around me. They were used to the old me. Change felt threatening, so they didn't necessarily resist, but they also didn't jump in to encourage either. So, here's the anchor: Expect resistance. Don't panic when it shows up, take it as proof people are noticing the change, and you're moving forward."

Daniel chuckled bitterly. "Rachel rolled her eyes the first time I paused before reacting. Like she didn't believe it was me."

"That's normal," Paul said. "Think about it. For years, you trained people to expect one version of you. Now you're teaching them a new one. It takes time." Then Paul wrote the following as he talked.

"Anchor: Anticipate resistance. See it as proof you're moving forward.

Work Examples:

- Colleague teases you for being 'soft'? Remind yourself you're not running their race, and they don't know what you know.
- Your boss doubts your new approach. Keep showing tangible results

and giving credit to the people involved by acknowledging the quality of the teamwork.

- Others question your motives. Reflect and make sure you are changing for the right reasons. And then move on.

Home Examples:

- Spouse rolls eyes at your attempt to pause before reacting. Stay consistent.
- Teen shrugs off your attempt to listen? Keep listening anyway.
- Friends laugh at you when you change the way you talk about 'those people'. Share something interesting you have learned about 'those people'.

And try this micro-action: Write down one place you expect resistance. Decide now how you'll respond without quitting."

Daniel's voice softened. "So, the pushback isn't failure?"

Paul shook his head. "It's confirmation of the ground shifting under your feet. Keep running the race differently."

Anchor #3. Reset Quickly

Daniel frowned. "But what about the times I blow it? I get sharp with Rachel, or distracted with the kids, or shut others down in a meeting. Feels like all the progress vanishes."

Paul's expression grew serious. "That's the old lie that failure erases progress. What I learned is that failure is just a stumbling block to overcome; it doesn't mean elimination from the race. The anchor is to reset quickly. Apologize fast, adjust fast, share the journey you are on, and then keep running."

Paul turned the plate over and wrote as he explained.

"Anchor #3: Reset Quickly. Failure is feedback, not final.

Work Examples:

- Snap at a teammate? Circle back the same day with an apology.
- Missed a chance to engage? Call it out by saying, 'I checked out there. Let's try again.'
- Don't be afraid to ask for feedback. Invite others on your journey by giving them permission to share what they are experiencing.

Home Examples:

- After snapping at your spouse, say, 'I'm sorry that was my stress talking, not me.'
- With kids, say, 'I overreacted. Can I have a do-over?'
- Avoid waiting for the perfect moment. Just do something and adjust based on what you learn.

And try this micro-action: When you blow it — and you will — practice the 24-hour rule: Reset within a day."

Daniel let out a low laugh. "Apologize fast. That one stings."

"It does," Paul agreed. "But it's the quickest way to prove the change is real. And in any situation where you fall short of your new standard, it is important to reflect on why you went with your old approach instead of the new. Knowledge creates the opportunity to choose differently in the future."

Anchor #4. Run with Others

Paul wrote the final anchor #4: Run with Others on the back of the plate, and as his tone softened, he said, "This is the one that saved me. You can't run differently alone. The Critic thrives in isolation. I needed John and my wife to remind me why I started. Relationships with others who know what you are trying to do to make the new race stick."

Daniel was quiet, staring at the plate.

Paul continued, "Accountability only feels threatening when we misunderstand it as a hunt for mistakes. But healthy accountability isn't about anyone tracking your failures. It's about inviting others into your growth so you don't have to navigate the journey alone. It's steady, supportive feedback that keeps you aligned with who you want to be. People may distrust accountability because of how they've seen it misused, but when it's done the right way, it becomes a catalyst for real connection and progress."

"Let's get this last anchor down on the plate. Anchor #4: Accountability fuels endurance.

Work Examples:

- Share one GENUINE practice with a trusted teammate and ask them to check in.
- Debrief with a team member each week and ask, 'Where did I show up differently? Where did I slip?'
- Share your motivations for change so others know it's not just what you are doing that matters to you, but why you are doing it.

Home Examples:

- Invite your spouse into the journey and ask, 'Where have you seen a change in me?'
- Tell your kids or friends, 'I'm trying to be more present, call me out when I'm not.'
- Don't be afraid to share your doubts and ask for support. Teammates are willing to root for each other; they just need to be aware of what they need to be rooting for.

And here's a great micro-action to get you started: Identify one accountability partner. Text that person tonight, 'Here's one way I'm trying to grow. Will you let me know how I'm doing with it?'"

The Layer Beneath

The grill popped, kids' laughter swelled, and Daniel's shoulders eased. But he wasn't done. "Paul, can I be honest? Sometimes I wonder if it's even worth it. My old way of running... it wasn't all bad. I built a career and provided for my family. Maybe I should just settle."

Paul set down the spatula. "I get that. I've asked myself the same question. The truth is, we all get pretty good at running the way we've always run — even if it doesn't give us the relationships or results we want. It's familiar and comfortable. But here's what I learned: Life is better with others, and relationships aren't a solo sport. I can't expect to get the benefits of great relationships if I am unwilling to do the things that great relationships need to grow and thrive. Changing how I ran meant retraining other people on what to expect from me, too. And that took time. Habits don't grow in isolated grand gestures. They grow in regular steps at a measured pace. Stay the course. Run at a sustainable pace."

Daniel nodded slowly.

"That's why I needed people around me," Paul continued. "Not just cheerleaders, but accountability partners. People who reminded me this was about lifestyle, not just behavior. Otherwise, I'd revert. And that is also part of the pre- and post-race routine John taught me."

Daniel was confused; he had never heard of the pre- or post-routines. So, he asked, "I haven't heard of the pre- or post-routines. Is that something for another plate?"

Paul laughed, "Ha, no way. John has mastered that part of the story and shares why he doesn't lead with them, so he will cover that ground with you when he thinks you are ready."

Paul wiped his hands on a towel, glanced at the grill, then turned fully toward Daniel. "Look, the Critic won't quit. The resistance won't disappear. The stumbles won't stop. But the anchors keep you in the race. Start small, expect resistance, reset quickly, run with others. That's how you build a lifestyle, not just a moment."

Daniel smiled faintly, eyes softening. "Run long, not just fast."

Paul grinned back. "Exactly."

Later that evening, after the last burger was eaten and the laughter of neighbors faded, Daniel sat in his car waiting for Rachel and the kids to join him, replaying the conversation in his head. Something about Paul's words felt different. They weren't lofty speeches or impossible ideals. They were lived-in truths, learned the hard way. They were practical tips for staying the course. Something had shifted. He no longer felt discouraged by imperfect progress — he learned some new anchors now. And, maybe, just maybe, the race was one he could actually see through to the end.

John's phrase echoed in his memory — "Run the race differently." For the first time, Daniel realized that meant not just recovering when he falls but staying the course when it gets hard.

A Quick Reflection

The next morning, while sitting in the driveway before leaving for work, Daniel grabbed the plate he brought home from the cookout and re-read what was written on it. He had no intention of taping it or any of his notebook pages on the office wall. It wasn't a heroic declaration. It was another small, quiet, and daily step towards running the race in a more GENUINE way. Before he drove to the office, he pulled out his GENUINE Advantage notebook, grabbed a pen, and on a new page wrote down the contents of his paper plate.

As the engine hummed to life, he whispered to himself:

"Start small. Expect resistance. Reset quickly. Run with others."

The lessons felt more real, the race ahead felt a little less like a sprint and more like a marathon, not one he had to run to outpace everyone, but one he just had to keep running at a steady pace.

24

Passing the Batons: Creating the Relational Legacy

A few weeks later, Daniel and John sat at the café. It was quieter than usual that afternoon, a hum of low conversation and clinking mugs filling the space. John leaned back in his chair; his hands wrapped around a cup of coffee gone lukewarm. Across the table, Daniel shifted uneasily, eyes darting between his phone and the window as if either might provide an escape from the conversation. He was struggling with all the changes he was trying to make in this new race he was attempting to run.

John let the silence stretch. He had learned long ago that sometimes the most powerful words weren't spoken quickly. After a pause that forced the heart to settle, he set his mug down and spoke with a steady calm that had disarmed men like Daniel before.

"You know, Daniel, when Paul first came to me, he looked a lot like you did when we first met."

Daniel blinked. "What do you mean?"

John nodded, his eyes distant, as he recalled. "He was worn down with restless eyes. His shoulders were tight with stress. He was running himself ragged trying to keep his business alive and his marriage together. He came into the men's group one night looking like a man about to snap. I could tell he was carrying more than one person should."

He leaned forward slightly. "All I did was walk with him. I didn't instantly offer to fix his problems. I didn't have a magic answer. I just reminded him that life isn't a solo sprint. It's a relay. You need to run your leg with excellence, but no baton was intended to stay in your fist forever. There will be times when someone else takes it, carries it forward. That's how it was designed to work."

Daniel sat back, crossing his arms. "And Paul... he figured it out?"

"Not overnight," John admitted with a faint smile. "There were nights he wanted to quit. There were times he stumbled. But he kept showing up, and over time, he learned to pace differently. He started listening to his crew, showing up for his wife, and actually being home for dinner. Small things at first. But they added up. And now—" John gestured with a hand, as if motioning toward Paul's unseen presence. "Now he's the one pointing others my way. Including you."

Daniel's brow furrowed. "So, Paul said I'm the next guy?"

John chuckled softly. "He did. But let me be clear, this isn't some exclusive club you got recruited into. This isn't about status. It's about stewardship. Paul is running his race differently on most days and is enjoying the fruits of that pace, but he knows it isn't supposed to end with him. The goal is to find others who would benefit from learning GENUINE. And one day, sooner than you think, you'll want to pass what you have learned on to someone else."

Daniel looked down, jaw tightening. "And what if I drop the baton during the exchange?"

John's voice was gentle but firm. "Then you pick it back up. Because the race isn't about perfection. It's about faithfulness. You don't have to run flawlessly. You just have to keep carrying what matters... and make sure it doesn't end with you."

Wrestling with the Idea

That night, Daniel lay awake staring at the ceiling fan spinning slowly above him. John's words echoed in his mind like a drumbeat: "Make sure it doesn't end with you."

The Critic appeared at the edge of the bed in immaculately pressed pajamas.

"Really, Daniel? You? Passing on wisdom?" The Critic's voice was smooth; venom wrapped in silk. *"You still mess up all the time. You have barely figured any of this out; how can you invest in someone else when you are still in debt? But now you think you've got a baton worth handing off?"*

Daniel squeezed his eyes shut.

"You've got nothing to pass down," the Critic pressed. *"You're still failing upward. And if you try to lead someone else right now, you'll just drag them down with you."*

The words stung because they weren't entirely false. He did feel unqualified. He had failed more times than he cared to admit. And yet... John's calm voice cut through the haze: "It's not about perfection. It's about faithfulness."

Daniel rolled to his side, willing himself to sleep. But deep down, he knew the question wouldn't go away: "Who am I supposed to invest in to carry this knowledge forward?"

Paul's Confirmation

Later that week, after the men's group had dismissed, Daniel found himself walking to the parking lot alongside Paul. The cool night air carried the smell of cut grass and coffee still lingering on their breath.

Paul glanced over. "I haven't seen you here in a while, but it was great to have you."

Daniel hesitated, then sighed. "I needed advice. John keeps talking about passing on the baton and about investing in someone else. I don't even know what that means. I am still struggling to keep my own head above water."

Paul chuckled. "That's where I was when he told me the same thing. I thought, 'How can I invest in anyone else when I'm drowning myself?' But that's the thing, Daniel, you don't wait until you're perfect. You just start showing up differently. Little things like listening when you would normally snap. Giving credit when you would normally grab it. Not showing up late for dinner one more night than usual. And before you know it, people notice. And when they notice, they have questions, which means you have something they think is worth sharing."

He stopped, placing a firm hand on Daniel's shoulder. "Don't hoard what you're learning. Someone else needs it. And they don't need you to have it all figured out, they just need you to be real."

Daniel swallowed hard. He wanted to believe that. He needed to believe that.

Paul asked him if he had noticed anyone who showed curiosity over his new approach to life.

One name came to Daniel's mind: Kara.

Work: Daniel Shares His Desire to Change

Two days later, Daniel sat at the head of the conference table, heart pounding as the client across from him aired their frustrations. A deliverable had slipped, and the room was tense.

Although Daniel was now trying to cover as much for his team as possible, he wasn't sure he had it in him today to take the blame. He glanced at Kara; he could see she knew the issue came from someone on her team, and so she was braced for the hit.

Instead, Daniel cleared his throat. "This one's on me. I missed the shift in scope, and it cost us. I'll make it right."

A flicker of surprise crossed Kara's face; apparently, this idea of Daniel taking the blame was still new in her mind. She didn't say anything, but her posture shifted — not defensive anymore, just... watchful.

After the meeting, as the others filed out, she lingered. "I'll admit, I was waiting for you to throw me under the bus."

Daniel exhaled. "You know I don't want to be that kind of leader anymore.

We both know your team missed the mark, but the client doesn't care who made the mistake; they just want us to make it right. They know me and know I am good on my word, so it seemed to fit."

She studied him for a long moment, eyes narrowed. "Well… it mattered."

At Home: Passing the Baton

That weekend, Daniel sat cross-legged on the living room floor, surrounded by Legos, while his son Ethan built a lopsided spaceship. Normally, Daniel would've hovered, corrected, tried to make it "better." But tonight, he simply watched, asked questions, and handed Ethan the next piece.

"Why don't you put the wings here, Dad?" Ethan asked.

Daniel smiled. "You tell me. You're the builder."

His wife leaned against the doorway, arms crossed, a faint smile tugging at her lips. It wasn't a grand gesture. But small gestures like this were becoming more common. Daniel wasn't distracted by his phone or halfway out the door. He was there. Fully. And that presence was worth more than the perfect spaceship.

Later that night, as he tucked Ethan in, his son whispered, "Thanks for helping me, Daddy."

Daniel kissed his forehead, whispering back, "No, buddy. Thanks for letting me."

The baton had been passed in the simplest of ways.

At Work: Building the Legacy with Kara

The following week at work, Daniel spotted Kara by the elevators. "Got a minute?"

She raised an eyebrow, skeptical as always, but followed him to a quiet corner.

"I know I haven't always had your trust," Daniel began. "There were times I deflected blame that should've been mine. But I'm trying to lead differently. And I have been watching how you lead. You're sharp, tough, and people pay attention when you speak.

Kara blinked. "Why pull me aside?"

"Because you're already carrying influence," Daniel said. "I don't want you carrying it alone the way I tried to. If you're open to it, I'd like to learn with you, grow together, and help you the way others have helped me."

Her guard didn't drop completely, but something shifted in her gaze — curiosity, maybe even the first hint of trust.

"All right," she said quietly. "I appreciate you investing in me this way."

Daniel nodded and said, 'You're worth it."

Reflection with John

That night, Daniel pulled out his phone and texted John.

"I think I found the person. It's Kara. She's sharp, ambitious, and doesn't trust easily. But I think she's worth it."

The reply came quickly:

"She is worth it. All people are. You've made progress running the relay and getting your team better aligned. I'm glad you found someone else who you believe can benefit from what you are learning."

Daniel stared at the words for a long time, the corners of his mouth lifting into a smile. He was excited to invite someone to join him on the journey. It would be really helpful to have someone else on the team who was focused on this new approach to the race.

Weeks later, Daniel sat at his desk after hours, the office quiet except for the hum of the air vents. He thought about everything he'd been learning — from John, Paul, and even from the conversations with Kara as he tried, awkwardly at times, to pass along the batons. He thought about the changes at home too: The extra patience, the renewed energy during playtime, the way Rachel often caught his eye with a faint smile when he was fully present. Their home felt lighter. More connected. Healthier. And as their rhythm shifted, he could already sense Rachel stepping more into her own passions again — not because he created space for her, but because they were creating it together as they learned to run this race side by side. For the first time in years, he wasn't consumed by the question, 'Am I enough?'

Instead, a new question anchored him: 'How can I continue to expand my reach?'

And as he shut down his computer and headed home, he knew the answer didn't have to wait for perfection. The plan was already in motion; it started with John passing it on to him, and now he was passing it on to Kara.

Legacy wasn't a someday thing. It was already happening.

25

Epilogue: Legacy in Motion

The community center buzzed with laughter and the clatter of folding chairs as families filtered out from a Saturday morning volunteer project. Kids darted between tables, clutching half-eaten cookies, while parents lingered in conversation. It had been months since Daniel had completed his lessons with John. He felt reflective as he leaned against a table, his son tugging at his sleeve, begging him to come outside and see the fence the kids had painted.

Rachel stood nearby, chatting with another mom, her sketchbook tucked under one arm. Daniel noticed the darkness of graphite under her fingernails — a quiet sign she had been drawing again. For years, he had walked past her buried passions. Now, seeing her sketchbook in her hand, he felt a different kind of pride — not the pride of someone who had 'made space' for her, but the pride of someone finally living in a rhythm where both partners had room to flourish.

Across the room, Kara stood in a small circle of younger team members from work, animatedly describing the next service project. Daniel caught himself smiling — not because she had perfected everything, but because she was leading with a steadiness he hadn't seen before. Where once she had bristled with skepticism, now she carried herself with quiet confidence.

A voice beside him broke the moment. "You see it, don't you?"

Daniel turned. John stood there, hands tucked in his pockets, eyes glinting with the satisfaction of a mentor watching the baton move forward.

Daniel nodded slowly. "She's going to be good. Better than me, maybe."

John chuckled. "That's the point, Daniel. If the next person doesn't go further, then we've only built monuments to ourselves. Legacy isn't about what you clutch. It's about what you release."

Behind them, Paul heard them and strode over, wiping his hands on a rag from moving tables. He clapped Daniel on the back. "He's right. John carried me when I was stumbling, but when the time was right, I passed it to one of my employees. He now moved out of town to help his sick parents, opened his own shop, and is about to open a second. My success feels great, but it pales in comparison to when he sends me a text thanking me for investing and believing in him. That's how this works."

Daniel glanced around the room: Kara surrounded by eager faces, Rachel alive with creativity again, his daughter surrounded by younger children tugging at her sleeve, as she teaches the rules of a game. It felt good not to feel torn between them. He didn't feel like he had to choose one at the expense of the others. Integrity had anchored him, generosity had opened him, engagement had focused him, and empathy had made him more aware of others. He was still running his race — but he wasn't running it alone.

His phone buzzed. For a moment, he considered ignoring it, but the name on the screen caught his breath: Mark. Just a short message this time:

"Seeing my boy tomorrow. Trying again. Thanks for not giving up on me."

Daniel exhaled; the peace of the moment was reassuring. His mind drifted back to those early morning texts from Mark — raw, bitter, defensive — when the marriage had first cracked. Every part of him had wanted to lecture, to say, "I told you so." But John's words rang in his ears, "Being non-judgmental means choosing curiosity over condemnation."

That choice opened a door. Instead of closing Mark out, Daniel had asked questions. He had listened. And slowly, the other batons had joined in:

- Integrity — showing up the same for Mark as he did for Kara or Rachel, not pretending he had all the answers.
- Generosity — reserving extra time and margin at night when Mark

needed to talk.

- Engagement — putting his phone away and really listening to Mark's fears about being a father who had already lost so much time.
- Unafraid — telling his friend the truth when he needed it most, but with vulnerability about his own mistakes.
- Empathy — remembering his own breaking point but letting Mark feel seen and heard.

One baton at a time, the door cracked wider. Slowly, Mark stopped talking about deals and started talking about recovering from regrets. He stopped posting rooftop cocktails and started asking if reconciliation was even possible.

And now, here he was — taking another small step back toward his family.

Daniel slipped the phone back into his pocket and whispered almost to himself, "Legacy in motion."

John heard him and smiled knowingly. "Exactly. It's not just about what you carry. It's about who you hand it to — and how far they can go once they've got it."

26

A Last Lesson to Consider: How Faith Helps Sustain Your New Pace

The house was still. Rachel's steady breathing beside him was the only sound, but Daniel's mind refused to follow her into sleep. It was one of those nights where, despite the progress, he still felt himself slipping back into his old way of thinking about the race. The ceiling above him seemed to stretch like a blank page where every unfinished task, every forgotten promise, scribbled itself in neon ink.

The Critic was back; he was less constant and less convincing but still around, especially at night or early mornings when Daniel was alone with his thoughts.

"You think a few batons change everything? What about the moments no one sees? The hours before the race even starts, when you still battle temptations to return to the old way? That's when it shows who you really are. You'll never keep this up. You'll always fall back."

Daniel turned over, pulling the blanket tighter. He thought of the meeting he'd led yesterday, which was much better than before. He was calmer, more present. For a few hours, it felt like he was learning a new stride. But now, in the silence of the night, that progress seemed flimsy. The temptations of returning to the old way of running were always present. No matter how hard he tried, he regularly felt himself slipping back into the same old race.

The sprinter's pace just seemed to provide more control and the perception of instant success.

By morning, his self-doubt hadn't lifted. He poured coffee into a travel mug while shoving his laptop into his bag. His daughter's voice cut through the rush, "Dad, can you check my homework before school?"

"I don't have time," he muttered, already halfway out the door.

Her small shoulders slumped. The Critic smirked: *"See? New batons, same old Daniel. You're still a sprinter. You can't change that."*

Later that week, sitting across from John at the café again, Daniel finally admitted, "I'm running differently during the day, but mornings and nights… that's when the self-doubt hits hard. It feels like I am always moments away from giving up or giving in and going back to the old ways of running."

He paused, stirring his coffee. "And if I'm really honest, something still feels off. It's like I'm running with people during the race, but before and after, I'm right back on my own. I can get through the laps, but when it's quiet, before the starting gun or after the handoff, I feel the Critic finding ways to interject about the good ole ways of running and challenging if these new ways are really all that good."

John nodded slowly, the corner of his mouth turning up. "That's because there is one more thing you need to consider. We've talked through all the GENUINE principles for how to run the race, but I haven't shared the foundational aspects of faith that help me sustain the new pace when I'm faced with challenges, and fight off my *Inner Critic* when he shows up. There are spiritual habits you can practice regularly to help you keep running the race differently and stay the course successfully. Without them, the race can wear you down, especially in the moments when you are lonely, tired, or afraid."

Daniel was a bit taken aback. "John, I thought I had the whole plan. Why didn't you tell me this sooner? I guess I am surprised by this new revelation."

John, as is his typical nature, didn't get defensive from the feedback; he was just matter-of-fact. "I don't start with the aspect of my faith because not everyone agrees with it. Some people even rejected the whole idea immediately. I used to start with the power of faith in enduring the race. I would preach to people that before you start changing how you run, you must build a strong foundation of faith. But that prevented many people from even considering this new way to run the race. I actually had people say, 'If that is what is required to run differently, I will just keep running the same way.' And that's when I realized I had it backwards."

Daniel wasn't sure if he was following or if he appreciated learning new information that could have been helpful from the beginning, so he asked, "What do you mean by backwards?"

John went on, "What I found is that when people experience you running differently, when they benefit from the experience of running the race with you, some of them eventually want to know how and why you run the way you do. And that is when it is best to share the foundation of your desire to change the way you run and how you sustain the change when adversity comes. For me, that was my faith."

Daniel still looked a little confused.

John had an idea. "Let's try a different sports analogy. If I introduced you to soccer, but I said before you can touch this ball or play a game and experience the joy of scoring a goal, you had to learn the history of soccer and the philosophies of the greatest players like Pelé or Messi. How many people would try soccer?"

"Not many, obviously," Daniel replied.

"Exactly, but if I gave you a soccer ball and said the goal of the game was to put the ball in the net using only your feet, now go and play. You might start kicking the ball. You will enjoy the freedom and simplicity of the game. Eventually, as you experience more and more of the game, at some point, you might get curious and ask about the history of the game or what you can do to experience even more success. That is when there is a desire for deeper knowledge, and I can explain the foundation of the game and the detailed routines that can be used (like dribbling practice, juggling, and drills) to increase your abilities.

Your interest in what I have to say will be higher because you have experienced the joy of the game. So, I adopted that approach in the way I teach people to run the race. Giving people the batons first is like giving people a ball and letting them play the new game. Some people will ask for more, and I share more, but some never will, yet their lives will still be better for having learned to run the race differently."

Daniel would have preferred a football analogy, but he couldn't argue the point that was made.

"Okay, so how do you apply faith to all of this?"

John Reveals His Pre- and Post-Race Routines: (The Anchors of Faith to Sustain the Race)

"Daniel, I need to let you know this is deeply personal. It's not theory, not something you read in most leadership books, but I swear by it. For me, the thing that made running different and sustainable wasn't just the batons. It was my faith. Without it, I wouldn't have had the strength to keep going."

Daniel tilted his head, reflecting on what he was hearing. "Faith really makes a difference?"

John nodded. "Yeah. When things got hard, and trust me, they got very hard, it wasn't willpower that carried me through. It was having the belief that there was a deeper purpose beyond the daily grind. That my desire to run differently mattered beyond just how it made me feel. For me, that deeper purpose was my relationship with God through Jesus Christ. And the routines that kept me grounded weren't just time-blocks on a calendar filled with randomness, but intentional time spent in spiritual practices—prayer, reading the Bible, and gathering with others who shared my faith. Those habits didn't just help me survive; they helped me continue to grow and refine the way I ran and my motivations for change."

He paused, then smiled gently. "I'm a Christian. That's the lens I use to view the world, make my decisions, and live my life. To ignore that part of my story and how it has impacted me would be hypocritical; it would be pretending I learned to sustain the way I run the race on my own strength. And that's simply not true. But many people would shut down when I led with my faith, so I changed my approach, not out of shame but out of love. I want others to experience a better and more fulfilling life, and the batons and their anchors are a huge part of experiencing a different way to run the race with different outcomes. So, the batons might be enough for some."

John continued, "But for me, my faith gave me the foundation I needed to not only make big changes and grow into the man I am now, but it has also helped me sustain the race and persevere when things got hard. It kept me honest when I wanted to hide. It convicted me when I made unwise choices, and it grew my ability to forgive and have empathy for others. It kept me humble when I thought I had all the answers. And it gave me hope when everything felt like it was falling apart."

Daniel leaned forward, thoughtful. "So, you're saying faith is essential?"

John noticed Daniel's notebook on the table, so he pulled it toward him, flipped to a new page, and wrote each of the words that make up the GENUINE principles vertically down the page, and then drew a line horizontally below the last principle and wrote the words: Spirituality and Faith below that line. Then he said, "I'd put it this way: It matters tremendously to have spirituality that's active and intentional. Belief in something beyond yourself. Because if you're only drawing from your own tank, you'll eventually run dry. My tank ran dry plenty of times. But prayer, worship, fellowship, and Scripture kept me connected to something greater, Someone greater."

Then, with a note of honesty, John added, "Now, here's where I need to be fair. I haven't tried every faith or spiritual tradition. I can't speak for Buddhism, Islam, Judaism, or any other path. I can only tell you what helped me stay the course and transformed me personally. Christianity did. Jesus lived out the very principles we've been talking about— generosity, engaged, nice, being unafraid, integrity, non-judgmental, and empathy. He mastered the art of relationships in ways that drew people in and changed lives for the better. That's where the batons I've handed you come from. They're not just abstract ideas—they're anchored in how Jesus lived and told us how to live, too."

Daniel nodded slowly. "But this book isn't really a theology lesson, is it?"

John smiled. "Not at all. This isn't about preaching a religion. It's about helping people run a better race by making relationships a priority, not an afterthought. If someone reading this has another faith, or even if they're just exploring spirituality, I'd still urge them to develop a routine that builds energy, creates purpose, and gives them confidence that running the race differently matters. There is a lot of research available on the value of Spirituality and religious practices, so I stand firm that they are an important part of sustaining the new pace. My personal experience with Christianity is that those values help, not hinder, running a new way.

We all have a set of beliefs that guide us; some people are just more intentional about establishing and nurturing them than others. Wisdom is using your beliefs to ground you, remind you of your purpose, and draw you back to what matters when life gets messy. For me, that's following Jesus. For others, it might be another way. But without something deeper, we're all just sprinting until we run out of gas."

He leaned in, voice quiet but steady. "So, Daniel, when things get hard—and they will—the best thing you can do is make sure your faith isn't just words on a page or superficial statements, but daily habits that shape you."

The Common Objection

Daniel rubbed his temples; the weight of what he was learning felt heavy. "John, I've got to be honest. This all sounds… good. But you can't bring faith into business. It doesn't belong in the boardroom. People don't want Bible verses in their project updates."

John nodded slowly, "I get it. And you're right, explicit faith doesn't belong in spreadsheets or strategy slides. I don't walk into meetings quoting Psalms. But here's the thing: There are lots of people out there who are trying hard. But most of them are trying too hard at too many things, which leaves them feeling empty."

Then he continued, "I was one of the worst. I was trying to run nonstop, all gas, no brakes, all the time in every aspect of life. And when the bottom fell out, I needed something deeper to rebuild my life. I realized that to run the race differently and sustain that new pace, I needed to reflect on and emulate the life of Jesus. And I can live that way without having to explain my motives behind what I do or proclaim my faith in every interaction."

Daniel sat in silence for a moment, weighing it. "So, you're saying it's not about dragging religion into business—it's about having a foundation outside business that shapes who you are when you walk into any room?"

John smiled. "Exactly. My faith makes me a better leader, not a pushier one. It grounds me. It slows me down. It helps me see people as people, not as tools to get things done. That's why I say it matters. And if you ask me, the life of Jesus is the best model of relational leadership the world has ever seen."

Daniel wasn't done yet; his voice was edged with something heavier than skepticism; it was personal. "John, I've got to be honest. I've tried the whole church and religion thing before. We attend the same church, and I am sure you've noticed I am not there regularly. But I'm guessing you probably have no idea why. But let me tell you, I've seen too many people use faith as a mask. Say the right words on Sunday, but on Monday, they're just as cutthroat and hypocritical as anyone else. It doesn't seem like it really makes that big a difference."

John didn't flinch. He let the words hang for a moment, then nodded. "I get it. I've seen that too. People quoting verses and acting the part, then being an unrecognizable version of themselves outside the building they call a church. That's not faith, that's performance."

He leaned in, steady and honest. "Here's the difference. Real faith doesn't give you a mask. It takes the mask off. It forces you to face yourself, the good and the ugly, and still say: I'm not running this alone. The routines I'm talking about — prayer, Scripture, community, rest — they weren't ways to fake it. They were how I stopped faking it. They kept me grounded when I wanted to hide. They reminded me I wasn't the center of the universe. And they gave me the courage to lead the same way at home, at work, and in private. No masks. Just alignment."

Daniel exhaled, his expression softening just slightly. "So, what you're saying is, this isn't about religion as a label. It's about spiritual routines that keep you real."

John smiled. "Exactly. If faith doesn't make you more honest, more present, more consistent, then it's not worth much. But the right habits, anchored in a belief in something beyond yourself, will help you sustain the way you run the race from the inside out."

Daniel let out a breath, half skeptical, half curious. "I'm not sure I'm ready to go there. But I can't argue with how I see you live your life. And I can't argue that the batons have made my life better."

John nodded gently. "All I ask is that just like you tried the batons mostly because I was persistent in checking in, consider trying this out, but it is a deeply personal decision, so I won't be checking in on whether you are doing them. All I know is I wouldn't be who I am without them, so I encourage you not to ignore the role of your faith in running the race well. Run the race, pass the batons. But when, not if, the storms come, you'll need more than your own drive to hold you steady."

Then John asked, "Can I at least share the groundwork of faith I built with you? As I said, I can't promise what it will do for you, but for me, without it, I'd drift back into the same old patterns. With my faith, I had spiritual habits that kept me grounded in the way I chose to run the race and steady in the headwinds of people and places that didn't always immediately appreciate my approach. There are four that changed everything for me."

Daniel didn't see a point in arguing, so he said, "Sure."

Faith Anchors for Sustaining the Pace

Anchor #1. Prayer

John folded his hands. "Prayer became less about fancy words and more about honesty. Every morning, before email or anything else, I'd sit in silence and give my worries to God. Sometimes I'd ask for wisdom or courage. Sometimes I just admitted I was tired. The habit wasn't about getting answers fast; it was about starting the day with perspective. It reminded me I wasn't running the race alone. I was inviting Jesus into all the details of my life so He could walk with me. So, anchor #1 is Prayer. Write that down below the line where you wrote Spirituality and Faith, and here are some examples for you to consider:

Work — Examples:

- Before a tough meeting, pause for a 60-second prayer: 'Give me patience and clarity.'
- Replace your first email check with a quiet reset: Offer your gratitude to God for one thing, and request wisdom on one challenge.
- Whisper a silent prayer in conflict, asking God for calm before you speak.

Home — Examples:

- Pray out loud with your kids before bed—even a simple thank you for the day.
- Begin dinner with a one-sentence prayer of gratitude.
- Use your commute to pray for your spouse, your children, or the people you'll meet that day.

And this is a good micro-action to try: Before your next task, pause for one minute and pray honestly about what you're carrying."

And here's an alternative: Mindfulness or a time of quiet to reflect and journal."

Anchor #2. Scripture Reading

John took a deep breath and continued. "At first, I was intimidated by the Bible. But I stopped trying to master it and let it master me. One verse a day—sometimes a single sentence—was enough. Words like 'Be still' and 'Do not be afraid' reshaped the way I showed up. Scripture became the mirror that reminded me who I was becoming, not just who I'd been. So write down Anchor #2: Scripture Reading. And here are some good examples to incorporate at work and at home:

Work — Examples:

- Keep a verse card on your desk as a reminder of your values.
- Read one Bible passage before work and let it guide one behavior that day.
- In stressful seasons, post verses about peace or endurance where you'll see them.

Home — Examples:

- Share a verse at the dinner table and ask: 'Where could this apply today?'
- Write a short Scripture note and tuck it in a child's lunch box.
- Read a Psalm together before bed as a family rhythm.

Here's a good micro-action: Choose one verse and carry it with you. Look for one chance to live it out before the day ends."

Anchor #3. Community of Believers

John's tone grew firm. "Just like we talked about needing to invite others to run the race in a new way, faith isn't meant to be a solo sprint either. I tried going it alone for years, and that's when I drifted the most. What saved me was a circle of men who knew my story and weren't afraid to call me out. We prayed together, we studied Scripture, and we told the truth. Without that community, I would have gone right back to the old race. So, add Anchor #3: Community of Believers. Here are some good examples:

Work — Examples:

- Find one trusted coworker who shares your faith and check in weekly.
- Ask for accountability on one behavior, 'Remind me to leave by 6:00.'
- Form a small prayer group for those who want it, without pressure.

Home — Examples:

- Join a small group at church where honesty is safe.
- Invite another family over once a month to talk about faith and life.
- Encourage your kids to build friendships with peers who share their values.

Here's an effective micro-action: Text one Christian friend you trust to ask, 'Can we check in this week? I need some accountability.'"

Anchor #4. Energy Management

John leaned forward. "This one surprised me, but it's just as spiritual as prayer, Scripture, or community. God didn't design us to run on fumes. If I wanted to experience Him, I had to manage my energy. That meant rest (Sabbath), exercise, and even joy. When I gave myself margin, I had enough to offer Mary, my kids, and my team—not just leftovers. Energy management is necessary to be your best. You are wired to gain energy through specific activities and routines. Find your patterns that help restore your strength and incorporate them into your lifestyle. So, write down anchor #4: Energy Management, and add these examples to help you apply it at work and at home.

Work — Examples:

- Block recovery time after big pushes instead of jumping into the next fire.
- Build rhythms of focus and rest—90 minutes of work, 10 minutes to reset.
- Use a walk or workout as prayer time instead of just squeezing it in.

Home — Examples:

- Honor Sabbath—set aside one day to rest, worship, and reconnect as a family.
- Prioritize sleep; your loved ones deserve your best, not your burnout.
- Do one life-giving activity each week that restores your soul (music, art, outdoors).

And here is an important micro-action for you: Identify one practice that recharges you and schedule it before the week ends."

John paused and then finished. "Prayer gave me courage. Scripture gave me clarity. Community gave me accountability. Rest gave me energy to make good use of my margin. Those four routines weren't add-ons; they are what make the batons sustainable. Without them, I'd have burned out or gone back to my old ways. With them, I could keep running differently."

Later that night

Daniel found the Bible he received in high school on an old bookshelf under a pile of other books he had enjoyed reading, but they hadn't really made much of a difference in the way he lived his life. But John's simple request to give it a try hung in the air more like an invitation than an edict, so he flipped the book open to a random page and began to read the words in red. What did he have to lose?

27

Author's Introduction to the Appendices

If you've made it this far, you've journeyed through everything I've come to understand about what it means to live a life well-lived — to grow personally, to build cultures of mutually beneficial relationships that accomplish extraordinary things, and to sustain quality relationships that make life meaningful.

You've also encountered a section on spirituality — because I believe it's the sustaining force behind our ability to learn, persevere, and ultimately run the race of life differently. It's the foundation that gives depth to our growth, compassion to our leadership, and endurance to our purpose.

The following sections are designed for those who want to go deeper — those who are curious about how the 'batons' form a relational operating system built on a foundation of faith, and how they can be used to intentionally shape a culture that lives out these principles.

- Appendix 1 explores how the *GENUINE* framework aligns with and is supported by the Christian Bible — offering a lens through which these relational truths connect to spiritual wisdom.
- Appendix 2 provides a high-level summary of what it takes to transform culture and why relationships are the cornerstone of sustaining meaningful change.

In this final section, I'll also invite you to see yourself across three dimensions — the personal, the relational, and the cultural — because true transformation happens when all three align.

Thank you for engaging with my story, and I hope it helps you on your journey.

Jonathan Couser

Connect with me on LinkedIn and at archimpacts.com. Explore tools and resources or join a GENUINE Community at genuineadvantagebook.com.

28

Appendix: A Deeper Look at The Spiritual Roots of the GENUINE Model

The plates had been cleared, and the kids were sent off to play in the other room. The house had that post-dinner quiet — mugs of coffee steaming, low lamplight, and the notebook, now worn soft from Daniel's constant use, spread across the center of John and Mary's table.

Rachel glanced at it. The seven batons stacked down the side in John's handwriting, and the spiritual anchors written below. They weren't just words; they had shaped the last months of Daniel's life.

She broke the silence. "I've been watching this unfold. Daniel is different. He's more present, softer even, but also... stronger. And I'm grateful. Daniel mentioned the spiritual routines related to Scripture and faith, and how you designed the batons based on the life of Jesus. But can you share more?"

John looked at Mary and smiled before answering. "I'm glad you asked. Here's how I've found it lands best for me: These batons are good for leadership and for living a life of love for others that builds community. But at their core, they're also discipleship. They're Scripture in action. Paul says in 1 Corinthians 11:1, 'Follow me as I follow Christ.' That's what these batons really are — patterns of life we saw perfectly in Him, now handed off to us."

Daniel leaned back, folding his arms. "I have been trying your spiritual routines, but man, they are way more difficult for me than the other real-life stuff."

Mary leaned in gently. "Daniel, that is exactly where grace meets you. If you could carry all this perfectly, you wouldn't need Jesus. But He doesn't call you to perfection — He calls you to faithfulness, one step, one handoff at a time. Remember 2 Corinthians 12:9: 'My grace is sufficient for you, for my power is made perfect in weakness.' That's what makes the race possible. You're not carrying these batons alone."

Integrity As Wholeness

John tapped the baton of Integrity in the notebook. "Integrity comes first because it's about wholeness. Proverbs 11:3 says, "The integrity of the upright guides them, but the crookedness of the treacherous destroys them." Integrity means the inside matches the outside. Who you are at work, at home, at church — one person, not three masks."

Daniel groaned. "That's exactly what I am working on. I lived like three people. At work, I was the hustler. At home, I was the tired dad. At church, I'm the guy who pretended to have it together when I showed up. I have been trying to close the gap, but I keep slipping back into compartments. Where is the guidance about not being split?"

Mary smiled sadly. "You don't stop by force of will. You stop by abiding. Jesus said, 'Abide in me, and I in you' (John 15:4). Integrity isn't muscling yourself into consistency. It's letting the Holy Spirit integrate you into wholeness. The more you let Him shape you, the less you need masks."

Rachel reached over and squeezed Daniel's hand. "And I notice the difference when you even try. Do you remember when the dishwasher overflowed last week? Normally, you'd shrug it off and blame the kids for loading it wrong. But instead, you admitted you'd rushed it. The kids laughed, and the tension broke."

Rachel continued, "That's integrity, Daniel. At home, you're the same dad in the kitchen as you are the boss in the office. Just like when you told me you took the hit for Chris at work because he copied and pasted something from you that was wrong, and instead of blaming him for not checking your work, you took responsibility for sending him the wrong information."

John added, "And in the community, it looks the same. There was a season when our neighbor only saw me in a suit and tie, rushing to the airport. When she finally caught me at the mailbox, I was curt and too busy to talk. That told her something about my priorities. But now, if she sees me in the yard, I make space. I want her to know she's getting the same John my church does, the same John Mary does. That's the real test."

Daniel sighed, but his shoulders softened. "So, integrity isn't about perfection; it's about showing up the same man everywhere, and because I am a Christian, that same man should be modeled after the life of Jesus. And when I fall short, I can turn to the Holy Spirit to guide me back to the right track?"

Rachel jumped in, "I think that would be an excellent place to start. We all mess up and will for the rest of our lives. So, we will need to rely on the power of the Spirit to get back on track as quickly as possible."

Rachel reached over and squeezed Daniel's hand. "And I will keep paying attention to the difference when you try. You don't have to arrive. You will never always get it right, but I see the effort and love the progress."

Generosity as Grace

John underlined the second baton of Generosity. "Jesus said, 'Freely you have received; freely give' (Matt. 10:8). Grace is generosity embodied — God gives without expecting repayment. We mirror Him when we give time, attention, encouragement, and credit to others."

Daniel sighed, but this time with a knowing weight. "That's still where the Critic gets the loudest. I've heard his voice for years — every time I give Kara credit, delegate responsibility, or slow down to listen, I hear, 'You're losing ground. They'll pass you. You'll fade into the background.' I know by now that voice is lying, but it still flares up."

John nodded. "And yet you've seen the fruit through the results you're getting, haven't you? Kara respects you more. The team leans in more.

That's the upside-down kingdom at work. Jesus said, 'Whoever wants to be great among you must be your servant.' (Mark 10:43) You've been learning that generosity doesn't diminish you, it grows trust and multiplies others."

Mary leaned forward. "And it's not just at work. Generosity also means giving generously at home, too. Daniel, Rachel told me you stayed up late helping her finish her portfolio for the art show she has been putting off for years. Your presence mattered to her. That wasn't just a task; it was generosity. You gave, not only your time, but your attention, too."

Rachel's voice softened. "And I felt it. It wasn't about artwork; I know you don't have an eye for art. It was about knowing you were willing to carry the weight with me instead of leaving me alone in it. That generosity gave me strength."

John added, "And in the community, it shows up in the same quiet ways. Last winter, when the snow piled up, our men's group shoveled a widow's driveway before dawn. She told us later that it wasn't the clear driveway that meant the most; it was realizing someone thought of her. Generosity always whispers the same truth, 'You are not forgotten.'"

Daniel looked back at the notebook with the second baton etched in ink. "I've been chasing wealth, influence, and achievement for so long. But I've seen now — generosity isn't about accumulating more wealth. It's about showing up with open hands, wherever God places me."

John grinned. "Exactly. Scarcity tells us to hold tight. Generosity tells us to give freely because God will provide. You already know which voice brings life. The question is, which one will you keep trusting?"

The added benefit of focusing on generosity is that it silences the Critic in a way nothing else can. The Critic feeds on fear; fear of falling behind, fear of losing control, fear of being unseen. But gratitude undercuts every one of those fears.

When you practice gratitude, your heart shifts from scarcity to sufficiency. From competition to connection. From earning to receiving.

John leaned forward. "Gratitude rewires your instincts. When you thank God for what you have, you stop clinging to what you fear losing. When you thank others for who they are, you stop viewing them as threats. Gratitude is the spiritual antidote to insecurity.

This is why Paul wrote:

'And God is able to bless you abundantly, so that in all things at all times... You will abound in every good work' (2 Corinthians 9:8).

Paul wasn't teaching passivity," John continued. "He was teaching confidence. Gratitude reminds you that God is not stingy. He isn't asking you to give from emptiness; He's filling you so you can overflow. When you trust that, generosity stops feeling like losing ground. It becomes an expression of faith."

Daniel felt something loosen in his chest—something that had been tight for years. He realized generosity and gratitude weren't two separate virtues.

They were two sides of the same transformation. One opened his hands.

The other opened his heart.

Engagement As Presence

Mary leaned forward while pointing to the next baton. "Engagement may be the simplest but hardest baton. Jesus never multitasked people. With the woman at the well, with the children who ran to Him — He gave them His undivided attention. Luke tells us that people were bringing their infants to Jesus, and although the disciples rebuked them for doing this, Jesus told them not to keep the children away (Luke 18:15-16). He never brushed people aside. Engagement is presence. It's honoring the image of God in each person who's in front of you."

Daniel nodded slowly, a rueful smile tugging at his mouth. "That one keeps catching me. I've already seen how costly distraction can be with Rachel and the kids. I'll be at the dinner table scrolling on my phone under the table, thinking I'm pulling it off. But I feel the shame and the distance. And they feel it too. It's not new to me, but every time I notice it, it still stings."

Rachel's voice cracked. "And I feel it too. But I also feel it when you put the phone down. When you lean in, even for ten minutes, the whole atmosphere shifts. It's like the evening breathes again."

Mary smiled at her. "See? That's the fruit. The Apostle Paul says, 'Look carefully then how you walk, not as unwise but as wise, making the best use of the time, because the days are evil' (Eph. 5:15-16). You've been learning that engagement isn't about volume — it's about focus. Presence, not just proximity."

Daniel's eyes glanced at the notebook. "And I've seen it at work too. Engagement isn't about being available to everyone every second. It's more about being fully there when it matters. When I step away from constant notifications, I think I'm failing... but the truth is, the times I've muted my phone, nothing collapsed. It's knowing what things are most important in the moment and choosing the best person equipped to handle the things I can't get to."

John tapped the table. "And that's the paradox you've been living. You think engagement costs you ground, but it actually builds trust. It reminds me of Nehemiah — when his enemies tried to pull him away from rebuilding the walls of Jerusalem, he said, 'I am doing a great work, and I cannot come down' (Neh. 6:3). Because he stayed focused, Jerusalem was fortified with protection. Kara grows, your team grows, and people believe in your leadership more because you choose to stay focused on what matters most."

Rachel added softly. "And it's the same here at home. The nights you close the laptop and walk outside with us, even if it's just for a short loop around the block, the kids light up. They don't measure you by the number of hours, Daniel. They measure you by how present you are in the moments."

Daniel swallowed hard. "I know. And that's the part that hurts. I've given them scraps of attention and excused it by saying I was tired or busy. But they don't want scraps. They want me fully."

Mary's eyes softened. "And in community, it's no different. It's the neighbor whose fence you help repair, the conversation you linger in, the pause that says, 'I see you.' The Apostle Paul says, 'Let each of you look not only to his own interests, but also to the interests of others' (Phil. 2:4). That's engagement — giving your attention away for someone else's good."

Daniel smirked faintly. "So, whether it's fences, phone calls, or family dinners, it's all the same test. Am I really present, or half a person in three places at once?"

John chuckled. "Exactly. Engagement doesn't ask where you are. It asks if you're fully there. Like Jesus told Martha, 'You are worried and upset about many things, but only one thing is necessary' (Luke 10:41-42). Mary chose presence. That's the baton."

Rachel's eyes met his. "And that's what I've been longing for. Not more time, more presence."

Daniel reached for her hand, conviction and tenderness in his tone. "It makes sense, but is so hard, the world seems to demand more of my attention no matter the cost, and work is a place full of Marthas worried about everything all the time. It is so easy to get caught up in that perspective."

John nodded. "You are right, that is why you need to build your foundation on solid ground, so you can stand tall in the midst of the pressure to conform to the world's standards."

Empathy as a Form of Incarnation

John pointed to the next baton and said, "Empathy. 'The Word became flesh and made his dwelling among us,' as it says in John 1:14. Jesus didn't stay distant — He stepped into our world. Hebrews reminds us, 'We do not have a high priest who is unable to empathize with our weaknesses' (Heb. 4:15). Empathy is a form of incarnation.

"That's the model," John said softly. "Empathy is incarnational in spirit. We can't replicate the Incarnation of Jesus; only God can take on flesh to redeem the world. But we can mirror its posture. When we choose to enter another person's experience instead of analyzing it from a distance, we practice a small reflection of what Jesus did for us."

"Empathy means stepping into someone else's shoes the way Christ stepped into ours. It means slowing down enough to feel what they feel, not just to fix what they face. That's how the divine love that entered our world through Him continues to enter the world through us."

Daniel thought about that. Maybe empathy wasn't just about understanding; it was about presence and showing up in someone's story with humility and compassion.

Daniel sat quietly for a moment, turning the idea over in his mind. Empathy as a form of incarnation. He wasn't sure he'd ever thought of it that way — that stepping into someone else's world could be an act of worship, not weakness.

He remembered when one of his employees, Claire, had started slipping on deadlines. The old him would have tightened control, but instead, he paused and asked, "Are you okay?" She told him she had a flat tire on the way to work, and her spare was also flat. So, she got stuck waiting for the tow truck. There was nothing to fix. So, he listened and let her express her frustration. Then he offered to clear her schedule, so she had the time to get the work back on track.

He hadn't considered that empathy wasn't focused on solving someone's pain; it was about stepping into it, so they didn't walk alone. That's what Jesus did. He entered our world, our weakness, our weariness, and stayed close.

Daniel smiled faintly, whispering, "'The Word became flesh.' Maybe every time we choose to show up instead of step away, His Word becomes flesh again through us."

Daniel continued, "I can see this, but honestly, sometimes I don't want to feel what others feel — it's like I'm carrying their weight on top of mine."

Mary leaned closer. "That's why Galatians says, 'Bear one another's burdens, and so fulfill the law of Christ' (Gal. 6:2). You've been learning this already — empathy is costly. But love is costly. And every time you enter someone's burden, it transforms them, and it transforms you."

Daniel nodded slowly. "So, empathy isn't weakness. It's actually the strongest thing I can do to fulfill the law of Christ. But it takes more out of me than I expect."

John smiled. "Exactly. It builds the bridge before you try to cross it. And you've been building those bridges, Daniel, one interaction at a time. Eventually, you will offer support, as someone who is invited to cross the bridge with people, and not someone storming the castle and forcing your solution on them."

John continued, "That is something we learn from the life of Christ and the message of the Gospel. Jesus came as flesh to experience our pain before he took the ultimate sacrifice for us on the cross. He wanted to be our personal God, not a distant Savior, which required him to enter into our experiences. And although our emotions are difficult to manage, and running the race differently is a constant challenge, we can always rely on the promise of scripture that says, 'I can do all things through Christ who strengthens me (Phil 4:13).'"

Rachel, who had been quiet, spoke up. "I see your empathy at home, too. The nights when you just sit on the edge of the bed and listen to me unload about the kids or the house or my own fears — those are the nights I feel closest to you. You don't fix it, and you don't rush me. You just listen. That matters more than you realize."

Daniel turned toward her, almost surprised. "Even when I don't have answers?"

"Especially then," Rachel said, her voice soft but firm. "Because empathy doesn't demand a solution. It says, 'I see you, and I feel this with you.' That's when I feel most loved."

Daniel exhaled, shaking his head. "Wow, I'm so thankful to know my changes are helping you feel seen and loved. And yet, I still hear The Critic saying, '*Efficiency wins — move fast, keep momentum.*' But empathy keeps slowing me down."

Mary smiled. "That's the kingdom way. People aren't interruptions to your mission; they are the mission. And when you embrace that, you stop measuring by speed and start measuring by connections."

Non-Judgment as a New Way of Seeing

Mary spoke first as she tapped on the baton of Non-Judgment. "Jesus said, 'Do not judge, or you too will be judged' (Matt. 7:1). Being non-judgmental doesn't mean ignoring when people fall short of the target (sin). It means refusing to define someone by their worst mistake. Jesus constantly invited people into a new future — tax collectors, adulterers, doubters. He didn't condone sin, but He never reduced a person to their identity being the sin.

He always gave them a path forward."

Daniel nodded, rubbing his temples. "That's another one I keep stumbling over. My reflexes are still sharp and critical. With Mark, with Kara, even with myself. Holding back doesn't come naturally. But I've noticed — the rare times I pause and choose curiosity instead of critique — something changes. The room opens back up. It's not that the instinct is gone, it's that I've learned there's another choice if I slow down enough to take it."

Mary's eyes softened. "And that's exactly where grace shows its strength. Judgment is natural. Curiosity is supernatural. Non-judgment is asking instead of accusing, seeing someone as a traveler on the journey rather than a failure stamped by a moment. You've already practiced this, Daniel — and you've seen the difference."

John leaned forward. "Think of Peter. After denying Jesus three times, judgment would've called him unfaithful, disqualified, and finished. But Jesus didn't condemn. He asked a question: 'Do you love Me?' (John 21:15-19). That question ultimately reframed Peter's story and gave him a future. You've done the same in your own circles — you know what doors it can reopen."

Daniel was quiet for a moment. "That story's been getting to me lately," he said finally. "I used to read it as Jesus giving Peter a second chance, but now I see it's something deeper. Jesus met Peter in his failure and still trusted him with His mission. That's the mercy I need if I'm going to lead differently. When I remember how much grace I've received, it gets harder to withhold it from others."

Rachel spoke up. "I see it at home too. When the kids mess up, it's easy for you to label them lazy, careless, or disobedient. But the nights you've slowed down and asked, 'What happened? What were you thinking? What were you feeling?' They've opened up instead of shutting down. That's when you had the chance to guide them."

Daniel sighed. "And when I don't pause, I see it on their faces. It's like I stamp a label right on their forehead, and the light goes out of their eyes."

Mary nodded. "Exactly. Judgment freezes people in place. Curiosity gives them room to grow."

John leaned back, his voice steady. "And remember, James puts it plainly: 'Mercy triumphs over judgment' (James 2:13). That's the choice you're making every time you hold space instead of slapping on a label. Judgment pins people down to their worst moment. Mercy gives them a path forward."

John continued, "And it's the same at work. Remember Kara's misstep? If you had lashed out, she would have pulled away. Instead, you asked her what got her to the conclusion she made. That gave her space to grow — and you led from trust instead of fear. You've seen both sides, Daniel. You know which one breathes life."

Daniel chuckled wryly. "I can think of about ten other meetings where I did the opposite. Quick judgment. Sharp critique. And every time, the air got heavier. I've lived the weight of it."

John smiled faintly. "That's the Critic's way — quick condemnation. But the baton way is different. It doesn't erase truth, but it delivers it with dignity. That's how people change. Not through shame, but through space."

Rachel glanced at Daniel. "And it changes me too when you choose it with me. Like the night I snapped about the bills, you could have fired back. Instead, you asked, 'What's weighing on you?' I felt seen instead of scolded. That's what non-judgment makes possible."

Daniel turned toward her, surprised. "I didn't realize that landed so deeply."

"It did," Rachel said softly. "Non-judgment makes room for love. And honestly, it's teaching me something about faith, too. I used to think grace was just what God gave me when I messed up — but now I see it's also what He wants to give through me when someone else stumbles. When I hold back judgment and offer understanding, I'm not just being kind. I'm participating in what Jesus already did — meeting people with mercy instead of measurement."

John raised his mug. "That's it, Rachel. Non-judgment isn't about lowering the bar. It's about leaving the door open. And when you live it, you discover the race was never meant to be run alone. Remember, many people think Christianity is about judging the sinner, but it is really a story of how Jesus judged all of us worthy of love despite our sin."

Unafraid as Courage and Vulnerability

John's voice deepened. "Courage is the currency of the kingdom. God told Joshua, 'Be strong and courageous. Do not be afraid; do not be discouraged, for the Lord your God will be with you wherever you go' (Josh. 1:9). That wasn't just a battle command. It was a life command. Courage is needed wherever faith is required — in homes, in workplaces, in relationships."

Daniel's eyes dropped, his voice low. "That is one of the few verses I know by heart, but living it keeps stretching me. Vulnerability still terrifies me. Every time I admit weakness, I feel exposed — like I'm handing someone a weapon they could use against me. I've done it enough now to know it builds trust, but the fear doesn't vanish. It just comes with me."

John shook his head gently. "That's the Critic twisting it again. Vulnerability isn't ammunition — it's an invitation. Every time you've chosen it, Daniel, you've seen what happens. People lean in. Trust multiplies. Without vulnerability, courage looks like bravado. With it, courage becomes leadership."

Mary nodded. "Sometimes the hardest act of courage is saying, 'I was wrong.' That's leadership, too. Real courage doesn't hide behind perfection. It risks honesty."

John leaned in, steady but kind. "Think about work. You've been learning to trust Kara, but you still wrestle with the fear that people will see you as less capable if she shines too brightly. Courage with vulnerability is telling your team, 'I don't have all the answers — I need you.' You've done that, Daniel, and it hasn't diminished you. It's multiplied your capacity."

Daniel exhaled. "That's still so backward from what I was taught. Leaders are supposed to be strong, decisive, and confident. But I've started to see how brittle that kind of strength is. It looks solid until the pressure cracks it."

John smiled. "Exactly. Strength without vulnerability is brittle. Jesus Himself wept at Lazarus's tomb. He sweated drops of blood in Gethsemane. No one doubts His strength — but His vulnerability revealed His courage. You've been walking that same paradox."

Rachel whispered, "And it's not just at work. The kids need that too. When you tell them, 'I don't know,' or 'I messed up,' or 'please forgive me,' they don't lose respect; they gain it. They see you as real, safe to follow. That's when trust deepens. Like the other day when you admitted you didn't know where in the bible it says that the world will be hard. Then you and the kids spent time finding John 16:33 and discussing what that really means, ultimately that Jesus has overcome the world."

Daniel smiled. It felt good to know others were noticing his hard work. "I think somewhere in the Bible it talks about how iron sharpens iron. I think that verse means it takes hard things pushing against each other for them to be shaped into who they need to become. That takes pressure, heat, and repeated effort."

Mary smiled. "Exactly. That is Proverbs 27:17. And Solomon finished that by saying, 'so one person sharpens another.' We are called to be courageous with others. That sometimes looks like courage with vulnerability. Risking being seen for who you really are — and trusting that God, and the people who love you, will meet you there and help you grow into the man God wants you to be."

Rachel reached for his hand. "And when you live this out, Daniel, it doesn't just change you. It changes us."

Nice as Personalized Kindness

Mary smiled, then she pointed to the next baton. "Kindness is love with skin on. The Apostle Paul says, 'Be kind to one another, tenderhearted, forgiving one another, as God in Christ forgave you' (Eph. 4:32). Nice here doesn't mean bland politeness. It means personalized kindness — the thoughtful, specific act that says, 'I see you.'"

Daniel chuckled, shaking his head. "That one's almost fun for me. I've seen how it works. Donuts for the office, picking up Rachel's sketchbook when she left it behind, and helping with the budget spreadsheet. And yet, every time, the Critic sneers in my head: *'It's trivial. It doesn't matter. Real leaders don't waste time on this.'* But I've also noticed what happens — those little gestures shift the whole atmosphere. They carry more weight than I want to admit."

Rachel shook her head, her voice steady. "That's because they're not trivial, Daniel. They matter more than you know. Every small choice tells me you're choosing us. They remind me you're paying attention, that you notice. It's not about the donuts or the sketchbook — it's about people feeling seen. That's what makes it powerful. It brings to my mind that Bible verse from 1 Peter 1:22, which says, 'Love one another earnestly from a pure heart'. That's what you're doing, Daniel."

Daniel glanced down at the notebook, where the letters of GENUINE stretched down the page. He thought about a recent morning at work, walking in with a simple box of pastries. Kara had laughed, "Another big presentation must've gone well if we're celebrating." But when he shrugged and said, "No, it's Jamie's work anniversary, and I thought we could all celebrate with her favorite breakfast snack," the whole office loosened. The banter was lighter, and the team was more at ease. He'd felt it in the room as the team lingered together and didn't rush to their desks to eat alone: Kindness disarmed the grind.

John leaned in. "That's the power right there. Kindness interrupts the rush. It isn't about the cost — it's about the care. Jesus noticed the leper whom no one else touched (Mark 1:41), the blind man whom others ignored (John 9:1), and the children whom others thought unimportant (Mark 10:14). His kindness wasn't generic. It was personal. You've been learning to do the same."

Mary nodded. "Exactly. Personalized kindness says, 'I know you, and I value you.' Paul urged us to 'encourage one another and build each other up' (1 Thess. 5:11). And every time you choose it, Daniel, it changes the atmosphere around you."

Daniel rubbed his neck, thoughtful. "I've started to realize something. When I choose kindness, I'm not just trying to be a better person — I'm following the pattern of Christ. He paid attention to the people others passed by. Every time I slow down to notice or act with care, I'm practicing His kind of love. It's the Holy Spirit nudging me to see, not just my own resolve."

Rachel reached across the table, her eyes soft. "You've grown in this with me, too. The night you noticed my sketchbook and brought it to me — that meant more than you know. You were saying, 'I notice what matters to you.' That's worth more than flowers or gifts. You are living out that beautiful verse from 1 Cor 13:4, 'Love is patient and kind.'"

Rachel smiled faintly. "And when you choose kindness here, with us, it teaches the kids what the love of Christ looks like. They don't just hear it — they see it in the example you are setting for them."

Daniel leaned back, letting the words settle. He thought about how much his understanding of kindness had changed from a behavior he tried to perform to a posture God was forming within him. For so long, he'd seen kindness as something to do; now he was beginning to see it as something God was doing in him.

He realized growth didn't come from trying harder to be nice but from staying closer to Christ, the One who embodied kindness in every step, every word, every interruption. It was the Holy Spirit who softened Daniel's reactions, slowed his hurry, and opened his eyes to the people around him.

Maybe that was what transformation really looked like — not a sudden burst of perfection, but the quiet shaping of a heart that was learning to see others through the same grace it had received.

He exhaled, a small smile forming. "Lord," he thought, "keep teaching me to love like You do and make kindness my reflex, not my effort."

The Real Way to Race

John folded his hands. "Daniel, here's the truth. You've been told life is a sprint — out-hustle, outpace, outrun. But you know by now that's the wrong way to run the race. The wiser way to run the race is with people, not against them. It's a relay, not a solo marathon. You pass the baton; you help others succeed. And when you cross the line together, it's sweeter than any solo trophy. Like Paul wrote, 'Do you not know that in a race all the runners run, but only one gets the prize? Run in such a way as to get the prize' (1 Cor. 9:24). The prize isn't outpacing others — it's finishing faithfully with them."

Daniel sat in silence thinking through it all, but it wasn't confusion anymore. It was recognition. He had lived enough of the divided, frantic sprint to know it left him hollow. Now, after months of carrying these batons in one context after another, stumbling, realigning, trying again, he could feel the shift. His voice was steadier than before. "That's the race I want to keep running. I don't want to split myself anymore. I don't want to run alone."

Mary reached across the table. "And you don't have to. Christ already ran ahead. 'For the joy set before Him He endured the cross' (Hebrews 12:2). He finished the part you never could. What you're doing now isn't earning — it's reflecting. It is your faithfulness built on His faithfulness. You carry these batons not to prove yourself, but to show what He's already done for you."

Rachel squeezed his hand. "That's the life I want us to keep building. One race. One story. No masks. Not striving to earn love but living because we've already received it. Remember, Daniel, 'We love because He first loved us' (1 John 4:19).

Daniel looked at the notebook again, every baton inked down its side. He read them slowly, like a litany: Integrity. Generosity. Engagement. Empathy. Non-Judgment. Unafraid. Nice. They weren't abstract principles anymore — they were practices he had carried, dropped, and picked back up again. They were the shape of faith that is lived out. His voice was quiet, but certain. "Then these are the batons I want to keep passing. Not just to my team. Not just to my kids. But to everyone God puts in my lane. Not to earn anything but to reflect what Christ has already done for me."

John nodded. "Then keep running this different race, Daniel. And when you stumble, pick the batons back up. Because the point has never been perfection, it's faithfulness. And faithfulness, built on grace, is always possible. Daniel, the truth is, we will never achieve ultimate maturity here on earth. You will be in a continuous battle against temptation and the desires of this world. Sin will be ever-present and pushing you to give up your new way of running. That is why staying true to the spiritual anchors I shared is so vital. We need the wisdom of God's Word, the example of Jesus, and the help of the Holy Spirit to achieve small victories and daily progress."

John added, "And our inability to achieve full maturity also comes with another promise: That God won't give up on us. 'He who began a good work in you will carry it on to completion until the day of Christ Jesus' (Phil. 1:6). And if God will never give up on us, then we shouldn't give up on ourselves, or anyone else either. A race where no one gives up on anyone is a really wonderful race to run."

29

Appendix: Implementing the GENUINE Relationships Operating System

Most leadership and culture programs start strong. The slides are clear, the stories land, and everyone leaves motivated to do better.

Yet within weeks, old habits quietly return. It isn't that people don't care; it's that information rarely changes behavior on its own.

Real transformation happens relationally, through people who model, mirror, and reinforce maturity until it becomes the group's shared identity.

Throughout The GENUINE Advantage, Daniel's growth didn't emerge from insight alone, nor did it stick instantly.

It was relational.

He changed because he was surrounded by others at different points of maturity, each one revealing what the next step looked like in practice and reminding him of the standard the team had agreed to.

That's the structure every healthy community needs: People to learn from, people to walk with, and people to invest in. All of them are working together to hold people to the standard. This creates a natural ecosystem of transformation.

Three Dynamics That Drive Growth

1. Learning Up — Modeling Changes Us

We grow fastest when we stay close to people who already embody the values we're trying to learn.

When Daniel watched John remain composed under pressure or hold truth and grace in balance, it wasn't a lecture—it was exposure.

His mind observed, but his nervous system learned. He began to borrow John's calmness and composure until those traits started to feel like his own. Change at this level happens by proximity, not persuasion. It's how humans have learned from the beginning: By imitation, not instruction.

2. Leading Across — Shared Struggle Builds Strength

Peers shape each other differently than mentors do.

Daniel's friendship with Paul became fertile ground for real change. Paul didn't have all the answers; he had perspective on his own journey and struggled to stay true to the principles when work was messy, and life felt heavy.

Those conversations gave Daniel a safe mirror: Someone equally committed to growth but willing to admit when it was hard. Together they learned that maturity isn't a clean ascent, it's a rhythm of falling forward, processing honestly, and returning to alignment.

Among peers, culture spreads sideways, not by authority but by authenticity.

3. Leading Down — Multiplying What You've Learned

We integrate what we've learned most deeply when we start modeling it for others.

When Daniel began mentoring Kara, he realized that teaching forced him to clarify his own habits. To explain kindness, he had to live it more consistently; to model integrity, he had to slow down enough to examine his motives.

Leadership, at its best, doesn't reinforce power; it multiplies maturity.

Helping others grow completes the cycle of learning.

When all three dynamics are active—Learning Up, Leading Across, and Leading Down—something powerful happens:

The group becomes a living organism of growth.

Each person receives, reflects, and releases what they're learning.

Change stops being an event and becomes the air everyone breathes.

The Reflection Loop

Every relational system needs feedback, and reflection is a key part of that feedback loop. It's what keeps the ecosystem alive and adaptive.

Reflection is the quiet pause after the meeting, the moment of honesty after tension, or the question that keeps leaders centered:

"Did my presence build a connection or diminish it?"

Without reflection, teams drift into performance without awareness.

With reflection, they return to alignment faster.

Reflection transforms experience into wisdom—it's how a culture renews itself in real time.

GENUINE as a Relational Operating System

When these dynamics function together, they create what can best be described as a Relational Operating System: A set of invisible patterns that determine how people connect, recover, and grow.

Unlike compliance-driven cultures that rely on external reminders, a GENUINE culture operates from within. Its relational system runs continuously through imitation, practice, and renewal.

Traditional training tries to change behavior through information.

The GENUINE Relational Operating System changes it through interaction. It builds emotional memory: The kind of learning that doesn't fade when stress rises.

Instead of relying on rules or slogans, it relies on relationships that model the right response until it becomes reflexive. Over time, this system makes healthy behavior the default setting. People naturally move toward generosity instead of defensiveness, courage instead of avoidance, curiosity instead of judgment. They don't need to recall a framework; they embody it.

From Personal Growth to Cultural Multiplication

Once individuals begin living the GENUINE principles across all three relational directions—up, across, and down—the culture becomes self-reinforcing.

- New members adapt faster because healthy behavior is visible and contagious.
- Teams recover from conflict more easily because empathy and honesty have become shared reflexes.
- Leaders spend less time enforcing values and more time exemplifying them.

In this kind of environment, growth is never isolated to one person's transformation. It circulates. Each person becomes both a learner and a model. That's how maturity scales. That's how culture sustains itself long after the training ends.

Reflection for Readers

1. Learning Up: Who consistently demonstrates a quality you're still developing? How might you draw closer to observe and learn from them?
2. Leading Across: Who shares your desire to grow and is honest about the struggle? How can you build a rhythm of mutual reflection together?
3. Leading Down: Who is watching you learn—and what might they be picking up from your tone, consistency, or example?

Healthy systems keep all three relationships in motion. That's what turns a set of values into a living culture.

Closing Thought

Transformation doesn't begin in a training session; it begins in connection.

It matures through practice, honesty, and reflection. And when those rhythms circulate through a team or an organization, the culture itself becomes a teacher.

The GENUINE Relational Operating System isn't a program to install; it's the pattern of how people grow when relationships themselves become the classroom.

Next Steps: Bringing GENUINE to Life

If you've reached this point and are ready to take the next step, we'd love to help you turn these ideas into action.

If you're a leader trying to instill these behaviors across your team or organization, ARCH Impacts provides GENUINE Operating System Engagements—custom-designed experiences that transform culture from the inside out.

If you're an individual looking to strengthen your own relationships and reshape your personal operating system, we offer one-on-one and group coaching to help you apply the GENUINE framework in real-life contexts.

If you're simply curious and want to explore more about how relationships drive growth and performance, you can join one of our interactive workshops or dive into our expanding library of learning content and resources.

Whatever your starting point, you don't have to navigate it alone.

Visit genuineadvantagebook.com to connect, learn more, and start building what's next because genuine connection isn't just how you run differently, or how culture grows; it's how people thrive.

From there, you can

- Subscribe to receive your daily GENUINE MICRO ACTION.
- Download supplemental resources and tools.

All of these are designed to help you and your communities learn how to take actionable steps toward running the race differently, growing individually, building cultures of mutually beneficial relationships that accomplish extraordinary things, while sustaining quality relationships that make life meaningful.

About the Author

Jonathan Couser is the creator of the GENUINE™ Relationships Framework and founder of ARCH Impacts, where he helps individuals and leaders pursue lives of clarity, connection, and wholeness. After more than two decades in executive leadership within Fortune Top 20 organizations, Jonathan experienced firsthand how outward success can quietly erode inner life and relationships. His work is shaped by biblical principles and a belief that healthy relationships are central to how we love, lead, and live. *The GENUINE Advantage* reflects his passion for helping people align their daily lives with the values that matter most.

You can connect with me on:
🌐 https://www.genuinerelationships.com

Subscribe to my newsletter:
✉ https://www.genuineadvantagebook.com